PHOTOGRAPHY
-CREATIVE TECHNIQUES-

Exeter Books

NEW YORK

Editor: John Farndon

Designer: Eddie Pitcher

Production: Richard Churchill

First published in USA 1985
by Exeter Books
Distributed by Bookthrift
Exeter is a trademark of Simon & Schuster, Inc.
Bookthrift is a registered trademark of Simon & Schuster
New York, New York

ISBN 0–671–07399–0

Printed in Hong Kong

INTRODUCTION

Although mastery of the basic techniques is an essential ingredient in the art of photography, technical skill alone is rarely enough to make a good photograph. Occasionally, photographs *do* impress through sheer technical excellence. Most of the time, however, there needs to be a *creative* as well as practical input from the photographer. It is this spark of creativity that is such a vital and, at the same time, such an elusive element in the success of any photograph.

There is an old argument which says: no-one can be taught to be creative — you either have it or you don't. While there is some truth in this, there is no doubt that everyone can improve their eye for a picture and learn to use their photographic imagination in new and original ways. Neither is there any doubt that the discovery of new techniques and processes can fire new bursts of creativity in even the most jaded imagination.

This book is intended to provide the basic groundwork to help you develop your eye for a picture, showing how the photographic frame, viewpoint, cropping, and different films and lenses can all be exploited creatively; and how colour, grain and contrast can all be manipulated to create striking effects. It also introduces a range of exciting effects to act as a catalyst to your imagination. All the techniques are described fully and clearly but, throughout, the aim is not to teach but to inspire the photographer to go out and take pictures — which after all is what photography is all about.

CONTENTS

Chapter 1
THE CREATIVE CAMERA
Creative approach

As more and more of the camera's functions are automated, the value of technical know-how in photography is becoming less and less significant. Processes such as exposure and focusing still demand considerable care and thought but, increasingly, the emphasis is on a creative approach, not on technique. The good photographer nowadays is not a photographer who has mastered the intricacies of f-stops and ISO numbers—although it certainly helps—but a photographer who has developed the ability to 'see' a subject and photograph it creatively.

It is easy to underestimate just how important the ability to 'see' a subject is. Seeing does not simply mean identifying general subjects. Anyone can tell that a dramatic hurdle race or a beautiful sunset are good potential subjects. The skill of the creative photographer lies in seeing the subject as a photograph and exploiting the photographic frame to transform the subject into a picture. This skill extends not only to choosing the best viewpoint or

time, but to actually identifying the subject in the first place. A photographer develops the ability to see the world through selective 'photographic' eyes and can find pictures in the most unlikely, as well as the most likely, situations.

An essential part of learning to see creatively is using the viewfinder to help previsualize the result. This is harder than it sounds, particularly with cameras where you hold your eye close to the viewfinder because you tend to see the subject, not the picture. If you use a 35mm SLR all the time, it is actually very instructive to borrow an old Twin Lens Reflex or similar camera in which you look at the viewfinder from a distance. Looking at the finder from a distance, it is much easier to see the photographic frame, and see the picture not the subject. When using your SLR again, try to withdraw your eye to the same distance in your imagination and see the frame as a whole.

One of the first things that may strike you as you compose your picture in the view-

Truck in the desert *Pete Turner's photograph shows how two apparently uninteresting subject elements, a truck and a desert landscape, can be transformed into a powerful, almost abstract photograph by skillful composition. The low viewpoint and tight framing are crucial*

finder—and as you look at the pictures in this chapter—is just how much stronger simple images are. Indeed, it pays to reduce the subject to a bare minimum, cutting out all extraneous detail and concentrating entirely on the feature that prompted you to take a photograph. If it was the strong character lines of the old man's face that attracted you, close in on his face, or restrict the depth of field to keep the background blurred. If it was a colourful streetsign that you wish to photograph, use a telephoto to isolate it from its surroundings—unless, of course, they are crucial to an understanding of the significance of the sign. Plain coloured or blurred backgrounds are always better than detailed, multi-coloured backgrounds unless there is a very specific reason for photographing the subject otherwise.

Even if the image you want is actually quite complex, at least start by thinking of the simplest possible composition. And don't be tempted to include extra detail unless it really does contribute to the overall effect. The red and yellow roses in the background of your portrait may look pretty, but they will dilute the image and

Boss-eyed *Portraits of businessmen can often be dull and formal, but even the least promising subjects can make striking, original photographs if you are prepared to use your imagination. Again the viewpoint is crucial, but so too is the man's studied pose.*

make a much weaker photograph. If you think carefully about just what you are trying to photograph and think about how you can frame it to make the strongest possible picture, you are well on the way to creative photography.

Scan through the pages of the colour supplements and magazines and you will see dozens of good photographs—yet the majority of them are very simple in composition (though often complex technically). The advertising pictures in particular use simple backgrounds to focus attention strongly on the product. Even though your aim may not be to 'sell' a subject in quite the same way, these advertising pictures provide some useful lessons. They show just how important it is to be aware of what you are trying to achieve—what the 'message' of the photograph should be—to give the photograph

the maximum possible impact.

Analyze what it is in the subject that attracts you or makes you think it is worth photographing, and then think about just how you can capture this effectively. Use the frame positively. Use light positively. Choose your viewpoint positively. The striking pattern of drystone walls or any other pattern in the landscape will look best if you use them to make a pattern within the frame. The soft texture of a woman's skin is brought out best by soft sidelight—if you cannot alter the light, you may be able to change your viewpoint, or move the subject to achieve the right effect. In other words, think twice before taking your photograph, unless thinking twice means missing the picture, and if your first viewpoint is not quite right, be prepared to move.

Remember too that creative photo-

graphy demands an element of originality. Sunsets, for instance, are one of the most enduringly popular of all photographic subjects and they have, inevitably, become something of a cliché. If you are photographing a sunset, look for a fresh approach, something that will lift your picture out of the ordinary. Think about shooting the reflection of the sunset, for instance—in a puddle, in a window, from a wet beach—or using it simply as the background for a portrait by flash. Look for this fresh approach with all subjects.

Above all, it is important to remember that photography is a unique medium; it is not simply a form of instant painting. So there is no need to stick to traditional, painterly rules of composition, unless that is the effect you are after. Photography is a dynamic medium, with a distinctive ability to capture fleeting moments and it is worth exploiting this. This does not only mean using fast shutter speeds to capture action, or slow shutter speeds to create a blur of movement, but also using the frame and using composition to create the impression of a moment suspended in time—or exactly the opposite, whichever you want.

Shadow play *The shadows are well-observed, but it is the precise framing of the sunshade and paving stones that makes this picture. The photographer used the viewfinder to positively design his picture*

New York, New York *This picture of the twin towers of the World Trade Centre and the Statue of Liberty captures all the glamour and sparkle of this famous city, yet the main technique is actually very simple. With the camera on a tripod, a zoom lens is zoomed out smoothly while the shutter is left open for a time exposure*

Cyclist *Silhouettes often make effective photographs because they reduce subjects to simple outlines. By shooting against a bright sky and underexposing (or using dense filters), you can achieve silhouettes at almost any time of day*

Raking the rice *Rene Burri's picture of the priest raking the rice is simplicity itself—yet think how many other viewpoints there could have been*

Composition and cropping

No matter how photogenic a subject is, it will not make a good photograph if it is not properly framed—many otherwise excellent shots lose their impact because the subject occupies too small an area of the frame or is overwhelmed by distracting detail. Intelligent cropping, either in the camera or on the final picture, can often improve a picture considerably, and can sometimes transform it completely.

There are, in fact, two distinctly different kinds of cropping—the first is used to exclude unnecessary or distracting detail to improve the composition, and the second is more drastic and can be used to create an entirely new picture or interpretation of the subject itself.

Some great photographers—Henri Cartier-Bresson, for example—will not allow their pictures to be cropped at all. Cartier-Bresson takes exceptional care to frame his subject tightly, making sure that all distracting and unnecessary elements are cut out, and that the centre of interest is precisely where he wants it to be. In order to do this he crops creatively and decisively, not as an afterthought, but in the viewfinder at the moment of taking the picture.

Ideally, this is where all creative cropping should be done. However, most photographs are taken in far from ideal circumstances—news pictures and candid shots, in particular. In these cases, events may happen so quickly, that there is no time to do anything other than press the shutter and record the

moment. It is much more important to catch the winning goal of the match or the child's expression as he is presented with a giant ice-cream, than it is to achieve the perfectly composed picture. You can always crop out unwanted items later.

In order to crop creatively, you should be aware of the elements of design which are involved in the making of a good picture. Cropping can be used to emphasize or enhance certain design elements, or to diminish or conceal others. Even before you have pressed the shutter, part of the picture design has already been chosen for you.

For instance, the ratio between the width and the height of the frame is determined by the format of your camera. This may be the usual 3:2 of 35 mm full frame cameras, or it can be 5:4, 6:7, or even 3:1 in the case of panoramic cameras. It is easy to overlook this kind of restriction—some pictures may look better with an alternative format.

In just the same way, the fact that you have a rectangular picture is also a design choice—pictures need not be rectangular. If it is seen in this way, the possibility of cropping to many different shapes becomes apparent. Oval cameo portraits used to be popular, for instance, and many head and shoulders shots can be given an old world elegance by cropping to an oval shape. An action shot, on the other hand, may be given more tension with a triangular format.

With the standard format, correct cropping can be equally valuable. The

positioning of subject matter within the frame, and its relationship to the frame edge can have an enormous effect on the picture and its meaning. The best photographers are continually aware of this. John Hilliard, for instance, has made a series of four pictures, called 'Cause of Death' from the same negative. Each picture has been cropped differently to give a totally different meaning to the image, and yet each picture is basically the same shot of a shrouded figure lying on a beach. The titles are 'Crushed', 'Drowned', 'Fell', and 'Burned', and in each case the title represents the meaning given by a different crop.

While the frame can be positioned to exclude or include particular parts of an image so as to create a certain meaning, it can also be used as a compositional device in itself. A popular picture is one which shows a scenic view framed by an overhanging branch. This is one way to use a frame within a frame, a device which gives depth to the image. The eye sees the frame as a **window** through which the gaze travels to find another 'window' (the frame formed by the overhanging tree). Different distances from the viewer are established in the picture, and an impression of

Man and desert *Cropping out the figure would completely destroy the impact of this picture*

Trees *Cropping in different ways creates entirely different images from the same original picture*

more of the subject immediately outside the frame. This emphasizes quantity and power. A picture of a group of demonstrators in a large empty street makes them look rather lonely, but if you crop in close to fill the frame with them, they look much more powerful.

Once you are aware of the influence that the frame can have on your picture, you can begin to look for these effects through the viewfinder as you take a photograph. This will make it easier for you to do your cropping in the camera before the image has been decided.

The corners of the frame have a particular effect on the composition as well. A pictorial element that runs into the corner of the frame from the body of the picture gives a sense of movement, dynamism or power. Imagine a photograph of a golfer, with his club raised for action. Now imagine the picture with the tip of the club running up towards an upper corner of the frame. You can almost feel the strength and power of the shot. If you crop this sort of picture so that the club occupies the centre of the frame, you lose this feeling of dynamic action altogether.

A composition in which a visual link is made from the centre of interest to a corner of the frame is a particularly effective compositional device. Cropping can be used to move one or two of the frame edges to adjust the position of the corner. Surprisingly this method rarely works well if the link is made exactly into the corner, but is much more successful when the link just misses the corner, or stops short of the corner itself.

Use of the corners in this way is really a special case of the use of the diagonal line. Any line in a picture that is not parallel to the edge of the frame gives a feeling of movement within the picture. You can include more than one diagonal in this way to create a series of implied

Truck *A dramatic crop to one small area of the truck gives an abstract image from a 'standard' original*

depth is given. When this is used with other depth cues, such as colour and tone, a surprisingly three-dimensional effect can be obtained.

Understanding the way in which the frame plays its part in creating the illusion of space is essential if cropping is to be used as a creative tool. Although the picture of the scenic view framed with branches may have become a cliché, the same technique can be used much more subtly. A whole variety of objects can be used to frame the main subject—from bus windows to a lion tamer's hoop!

On the other hand, some subjects may have more impact if you crop the picture so that the subject fills the frame to the edges, whether you are cropping in the camera, or as an afterthought. When parts of the image are pressed up against the edge of the picture in this way, the impression is given that there is

Archway figure
The large dark area on the left of the picture dominates the image. Cropping into the picture in this way emphasizes the shape of the lone figure within the archway

and shoulders so that the animated expressions of the two combatants fill the frame. Many other pictures might be improved in this way, cutting out all irrelevant and distracting detail that might reduce the impact of the subject.

Remember, though, that it is easy to over crop. While cropping in close may simplify and strengthen the image, it may also cut out some important information and distort or devalue the picture. If, for example, the idea of a picture was to show George on holiday at the sea, it would be ridiculous to crop in on George and exclude the sea in the background. Pictures would also tend to look rather similar if they were all tight-cropped. There should ideally be a good balance between background information and the central subject in this kind of shot.

The exact position of the crop can be crucial. You can see the effect of cropping by experimenting on a full length portrait. Try covering up the picture gradually, judging the effect of the crop-mark—first just the feet, then the shins and so on. While information is lost as more is cropped out, the image becomes larger and simpler. Quite often, a full crop in on the head and shoulders can produce a completely different picture from the full length shot—it may even give a completely different impression of the subject—even though both approaches produce an attractive result.

The same can apply to many other subjects—landscapes, for example, can often benefit or give an entirely different image when cropped in a certain way. One thing to remember when cropping, though, is not to undervalue space in a picture. An empty space may not seem to contribute positively to the effect but without it, the picture can seem unbalanced. Try to use space as well as detail creatively.

Space can also be used to illustrate or emphasize action in a photograph. Moving objects retain that feeling of movement if they have a space to move into. A fast car, or a runner, usually photographs far more effectively when

movements within the picture. Gentle diagonals at a less acute angle are often seen in landscape pictures, where they add a lyrical quality to the image. More powerful diagonals clashing with each other give a sense of chaos and even violence to the image. However, the relationship between the diagonals and the frame is actually more dynamic than the relationship between the individual diagonals themselves. Sensitive cropping, therefore, can be used to tilt the frame slightly one way or the other in order to make the most of these diagonals.

It follows that lines which are parallel to the edge will have the opposite effect, giving a sense of stillness, solidity and strength.

Space is another component of a photograph that cropping can control. While it is always important to avoid wasted space in a picture, not all empty space is necessarily wasted space. The most obvious use of space is to convey the idea of isolation—a lone figure walking through a huge landscape, a child who seems lost in an empty street. Pictures like these need their space to work well. If you cropped to the edge of the subject, in these cases, you would lose the point of the picture. Cropping may well be used to remove

any other detail that might otherwise detract from this simplicity.

Although at first glance, there may seem to be little wrong with the framing of a particular picture, it is surprising how many pictures can be improved by cropping in a little tighter. In a candid shot of two people arguing, for instance, the original half-body shot may seem to be quite natural and pleasing, but the shot may provide a far more potent image if it is cropped in on just the head

Turkish gunman *A moving subject needs an empty space to move in to*

it is moving into an empty part of the frame, than if its line of movement is stopped by some other visual element in the image. Don McCullin used this technique brilliantly in his picture of a Turkish gunman running from a doorway in Cyprus. The space in this picture is given added strength since the shadow of the gunman emphasizes his movement into this bare space. There are clearly occasions when it is important for a picture to have additional space. In these cases, you must compose your photograph carefully at the time, for cropping after the event will not help.

One of the most difficult things to achieve in a photograph is a sense of rhythm. It is something that you can gradually become aware of, the more pictures you take. You can say a photograph has rhythm when it has achieved a balance between the forms and the space within the frame. In the Don McCullin photograph already mentioned, the relationship between the figure with the gun and the space he is moving into is repeated slightly differently in the relationship between the shadow and the space that it is moving into. This is further echoed behind the gunman in the way that the figure in the doorway relates to the space between the door and the gunman.

A repetition of similar, but different shapes and forms in a picture creates rhythm. Sensitive cropping can often be used to adjust the spaces or forms slightly, so as to enhance the rhythm in a picture or to remove something that

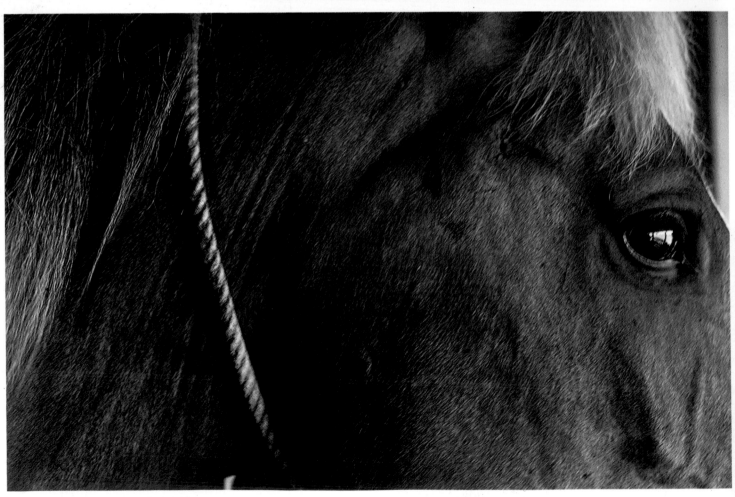

The process of cropping

The essential tools of cropping are fairly straightforward. You will find it helpful to use two L-shaped pieces of firm card, preferably black. The two pieces together create a boxed-in area in which you can compose the picture you want, excluding something distracting, or an empty area that contributes nothing.

While it is relatively simple to eliminate part of a black and white print, either by cutting off the cropped out area directly, or by cropping it off on the enlarger base-board when you make another print, it is more difficult to crop a transparency. You can use masking tape over the crop-ped out area, or you can buy a masking frame of a more interesting shape. Alternatively, you can have a duplicate transparency made which includes only the needed area. Until recently, this was best left to a specialist colour laboratory. Now attachments can be fitted to the camera to make duplicate transparencies with a different crop by using a zoom lens. The original slide is put into the duplicator and the camera focused on it. The zoom lens on the duplicator is adjusted so that the portion of the original which is not required is zoomed out of the viewfinder, and the new duplicate con-tains only the enlarged area of the picture which is needed.

Fishing *Here, a third figure was cropped out to improve the balance*

Bjorn Borg *The strong diagonal lines give a sense of dynamic action, while tight cropping emphasizes the service*

detracts from it. Used well, rhythm gives life and freshness in a picture.

Composition, therefore, is simply the art of arranging the elements of the picture—shapes, lines, tones and colours —in a pleasing and orderly way. In most cases a well-organized picture is not

Horse *A subject can often be depicted more dramatically if you crop right down to one strong feature*

On the grid *Tight cropping eliminates all distracting detail at the race track*

only more satisfying to look at, but it is much easier to understand. In a way, cropping after the exposure has been taken is an admission that you did not get the picture right first time, but only a purist would reject the improvement in strength and elegance that creative cropping can bring to those 'near misses'.

Only a few pictures out of the billions of exposures made annually become great pictures. While they may well be created because someone has been in the right place at the right time, they become great pictures because every element in the picture is important, and nothing is included which is not essen-tial—cropping whether in the view-finder or later, has been effective. It may well make all the difference to one of your pictures.

15

Viewpoint

Garden *The intricate layout of a formal garden cannot be fully appreciated from ground level so the photographer used an adjacent building for this shot*
Camels *An aerial view turns the shadows of the camels into an almost abstract design, showing why aerial photography has been such a significant influence on abstract art.*

Choice of viewpoint is one of the most obvious creative tools available to the photographer. Although it is an integral part of the picture taking process—simply the direction the camera is pointing in relation to the subject—it is also one of the easiest ways of giving more impact to a photograph. All too often people become lazy about looking for a viewpoint which is appropriate to the subject and end up with nearly all their photographs taken from eye level.

Most of us become totally accustomed to seeing our surroundings from eye level so that looking at photographs taken the same way is less likely to generate much impact. However a carefully chosen viewpoint might provide a strikingly unusual view—or it may offer the ideal viewing angle to appreciate the design of a house or an exotic car. This viewpoint need not necessarily mean an extreme—after surveying a location you may well conclude that eye level is actually the best way of photographing the main subject.

Angling a camera so you view your subject from below brings certain characteristics to a photograph. A low viewpoint can create an unusual juxtaposition—perhaps a close-up of a cricket ball in the foreground photographed from ground level with a game of cricket visible in the background. However a low viewpoint can also create a sense of power, dominance and menace. The power of a racing car is much more graphically conveyed by shooting across the car from its own level, or from below it, than from a high view looking down on to it. Similarly, a low wide angle shot of a famous personality—perhaps a politician—will convey more of a sense of their power than a shot looking down onto them. This is one reason why speeches are made from elevated stages. The low viewing angle adopted by Frank Hermann for his photographs of soldiers at drill, for instance, has a similar effect and gives the viewer a strong sense of the power and authority invested in the subjects. In this case it was not an extreme position—it was simply a matter of shooting from a squatting position rather than from normal eye level.

A low viewpoint can also be invaluable in a more pictorial way. It can allow you to give less emphasis to a featureless foreground—perhaps by using a wide angle lens and framing a landscape between some flowers—or even between some blades of grass. The

When photographing from a building or some other high viewpoint, telephoto lenses are often ideal for closing in for a bird's eye view of the people below. However, telephotos are also ideal for concentrating on the patterns which are often visible from above. The way pavements and roads are arranged, the lines on the road or a group of trees in a city square can all create interesting patterns that are rarely seen otherwise. In the same way, an intricately laid out garden will make a fascinating subject from above—such photographs generate interest from the viewer simply because what they see is such a departure from the normal view.

Many subjects lend themselves to this treatment—whether a view from a mast looking down on to a yacht, a bird's eye shot of a tennis player serving, or a row of swimmers competing in a swimming pool. Often, hazardous climbing exploits are unnecessary and it is not hard to find a vantage point once you have decided

exaggerated perspective which such a viewing position creates can also be used effectively. A classic example is of a road or section of railway line stretching off towards the horizon. A low viewpoint will make the convergence more dramatic and will allow the photograph to include details in the foreground such as the texture of the road itself. This technique also allows the eye to be led towards a significant part of the picture and is similar to the effect created by framing a shot so that a wall or hedgerow leads your eye into the distance.

In contrast, the opposite extreme—finding an unusually high viewpoint—also gives its own characteristic effects to a photograph. Try looking down from a fairly high window on to the street below. Pedestrians walking along or standing on street corners take on a very unusual appearance. This effect of a high viewpoint can be exploited with dramatic results. People or animals, for example, take on almost unrecognizable shapes when viewed from above—often the main clue to identifying the subject is provided by the shadow that the shape casts across the ground.

Low shot *By lying on the ground beneath the marksman, the photographer created a sense of menace.* **Modern architecture** *The convergence caused by using a wide angle lens from a low viewpoint adds emphasis to an unusual design.* **Rear view** *Here the choice of viewpoint created a striking image of a familiar subject.* **Tables and chairs** *A high viewpoint allowed the brightly painted objects to be contrasted with the surrounding foliage and resulted in this particularly striking image*

Café *A viewpoint need not necessarily be an extreme—here just crouching helped the overall composition*

Cat *Animals benefit from being photographed at an angle corresponding to a scale of their own world*

airline pilot, confronted with a huge array of dials and switches, are both examples of this. The view of a performer confronted with a large audience is another—and in all these cases the photograph gives a more involved glimpse into the world of the person concerned. Similarly, photographing a child from above imposes an adult viewpoint—a far more natural choice is to crouch down and shoot from the child's own level. The idea of a point of view can be taken a stage further such as by placing a camera fitted with a fisheye or ultra-wide angle lens inside a rugby scrum to give dramatic results.

Choice of viewpoint can often be limited by obstruction but in such cases it is often best to try to make a feature out of the problem. In a crowd for instance, why not frame the main subject between the heads of the people in front of you? If the subject is a house, surrounded by high walls and a gate, forget about trying to shoot between the railings of the gate and angle the shot so that the gate becomes part of the final photograph and frames the house in the background.

While there is plenty of scope for manipulating your viewpoint to create a more striking image, do not be diverted away from the most straightforward viewpoints on every occasion. A simple front or side view may be the best. The general rule is to check out all of the alternatives, and even photograph the same scene from as many vantage points as possible. You may find that each photograph is as effective as the others or your practical experience may teach you that some viewpoints suit a particular subject far more than others.

Washing *Even a subject as mundane as a washing line can be turned into something interesting by choosing an original viewpoint.* **Feet** *An aerial viewpoint once more creates an abstract design, but the viewpoint is less than six feet above the ground. Looked at in this way, even the most mundane objects in the city streets can make strikingly beautiful photographs*

that elevation would improve your view of the subject.

On a more practical note, elevated viewpoints can be indispensible for allowing yourself a clear view of the subject. A photographer may carry a small step ladder along to an event, for instance, so that he or she can see over the heads of others present and get a more unusual view of the proceedings—perhaps deliberately including the heads of those in front.

While high and low viewpoints each have their own ways of shaping the image, often the viewpoint is dictated by the subject itself. Using the camera from someone else's viewpoint—perhaps even photographing over their shoulder—is an ideal way of presenting the elements of a scene. The view of a train driver looking through his cab window out onto the tracks ahead or of an

Creative wide angle

In the search for a new approach in photography it is much easier to resort to a gimmick, such as a coloured filter or a distorting lens, than to think of a genuinely creative technique. It is a great pity that wide angle lenses, particularly of the ultra-wide variety, are abused so often in this way, when they have much more to offer the photographer than simply a wide, distorted view of the subject.

Most people can actually see over a wider angle than the widest ultra-wide lens, but only really notice a very small area. So a wide angle view can sometimes surprise and intrigue simply by including elements of a scene that would not normally be noticed. Even a moderate wide angle panorama of a broad landscape, such as a 28 mm, may include foreground detail or elements that people normally fail to see. A view of a sunset, for instance, may include a deep blue sky overhead, as well as the golden glow around the sun that held the attention in the original scene. With a standard lens, this rich contrast might have been lost. A snowscape, on the other hand, may include the texture of footprints in the foreground which contribute towards the success of the final image.

One of the most valuable properties of the wide angle is its great depth of field which allows you to include close foreground detail in a generally distant scene while keeping both perfectly sharp. A photograph which is composed in this way can draw the viewer into the picture, creating a sense of involvement. For instance, you may have, as your subject, a sideshow at a fairground where there is a small crowd of spectators. Instead of standing in the front row for an unobstructed view, or shooting from a higher viewpoint at a distance with a telephoto lens, try shooting from within the crowd with a wide angle lens, so that two or three spectators frame the sideshow on either side of the photograph. Anyone viewing the picture is made to feel part of the crowd in this way. In other situations you could use trees, a window, even a hole in the wall as a frame.

Apart from using foreground objects simply to lead the viewer into the picture, you can add considerable interest to your compositions by choosing these objects carefully so that you create a relationship between near and far elements in a scene. A foreground rock, for instance, can not only lead the eye towards the mountain landscape in

Windmill *The close viewpoint possible with a wide angle lens creates strong lines of perspective. These can be particularly effective pictorially when combined with clear diagonal lines across the frame*

the background, but also gives an idea of the scale and structure of a mountain. An isolated car in the foreground could make a background desert or open prairie appear more lonely and desolate than it really is.

Alternatively, you could use this technique to illustrate an idea or story— for instance, a single lonely seedling growing in the ashes of a forest fire, using the enhanced perspective of the wide angle lens to exaggerate the size of the small foreground subject. While wide angle lenses increase your view of the overall scene, at the same time they alter the effect of perspective in a picture so that the foreground seems to dominate the picture.

One famous photograph by Art Kane made excellent use of this emphasis on foreground. In a portrait of the boxer Joe Louis, Kane posed his subject with his remarkable hands clenched on his knees, and by shooting from a close, low viewpoint he made the fists dominate the image, as they had dominated Louis' life. In this case the photographer used the specific characteristics of the wide angle lens as a creative contribution to his subject.

In the same way you could position someone who is working at a potter's wheel, for instance, so that the wheel, the unfinished pot, and their working hands dominate the picture by occupying a foreground position. This is a particularly useful technique to use when dealing with shots of people at work, when you want to emphasize what they are doing, whether it is a portrait of an architect, a master chef or a child painting.

Clearly, to make the most of this effect, you need to choose your viewpoint with great care. A view from over a balcony, for instance, is unlikely to contain any foreground details, and so the sense of depth is weak. However, you can move your viewpoint so that the balcony forms part of the foreground, giving a very marked sense of perspective to the picture.

With a wide angle, small changes in viewpoint make enormous differences to a composition, and it is worth exploring each different aspect fully. You can, in fact, choose a detail for the foreground of one picture, and then, by moving around a little, choose another detail without altering your background.

If small changes in viewpoint make such large differences to the composition, extreme viewpoints, such as those given from the top of a wall, or from close to the ground, have an extraordinary effect. A wide angle used from the ground can make nearby people look like giants, for instance, or it can create fantastic landscapes out of a small piece of earth.

Quite apart from appearing to change the size and shape of the subject, the strengthened perspective given by a wide angle lens tends to produce images that have more pronounced diagonal lines. Compositionally, diagon-

als help to give vitality and a sense of popular in commercial photography when the subject has to be made into as lively an image as possible. You can pick out a minor feature, such as a path leading up to a church, a rope attaching a boat to its moorings, or the shadow of a figure, and turn it into a significant point in the composition as a strong diagonal leading the eye towards the main

subject, and sometimes striking right across the frame.

The range of compositional effects possible with a wide angle lens is enormous and the pictures on this and the following pages serve to show just some of the other ways their all-encompassing eye can be exploited photographically. But beware: the effects can easily be overdone and become just another photographic gimmick.

Aircraft *With a low viewpoint, an ultra-wide angle has a dramatically distorting effect on any subject*

Striped rug *A wide angle can change a foreground detail into a feature of significant interest*

Hotel *Even a moderately wide angle lens can transform a modest structure into a more impressive building*

Pumpkins *When used close to a subject, a wide angle enables you to fill the frame entirely, without a background*

Shells *The great depth of field of a wide angle allows you to include a sharp horizon in a close-up shot.*
Black hats *You can make an interesting feature from a wide angle's ability to emphasise foreground features.*

Lupins *A carefully selected viewpoint with a wide angle creates different angles from simple vertical lines.*
White church *The 'classic' wide shot—establishing a relationship between near and distant subjects*

Creative telephoto

Lenses of different focal lengths each bring their own visual characteristics to a photograph. Simply fitting a particular type of lens to your camera makes you think a certain way and look specifically for subjects which suit the equipment you have at hand. Telephoto lenses in particular have this effect—when you look at your surroundings through a telephoto, certain subjects present themselves more readily than others—a row of telegraph poles that can be compressed together, a patterned field that can be isolated from a wide vista or a solitary figure walking along an empty city street.

The characteristics of longer telephoto lenses—compressed perspective, shallow depth and a narrow field of view—become more distinctive with lenses longer than around 200 mm. Lenses of this group often allow you to create pictures out of the most inauspicious surroundings.

Most people fit a long telephoto lens for its most basic purpose—to magnify the subject so that it appears larger in the frame. As such it becomes a basic tool for candids, sports, wildlife and other subjects where the photographer's

Shower *The selective view of a long telephoto was exploited here to isolate the figures standing behind the curtain of spray*

Statue of Liberty *Striking sunset pictures can be made with very long lenses but they look more striking still if a bold silhouette is included*

access to the subject is limited. Many images fail to generate impact simply because the photographer has not managed to get close enough to the subject so that the main area of interest is not sufficiently detailed and so there is too much extraneous space around it. Long telephotos overcome this problem with ease—even in the most commonplace situations—perhaps filling the frame with the face of a stranger standing on the other side of the street. This facility makes you look for other subjects, rarely seen at close range—cloud formations, for instance, make interesting subjects when seen through a 200 or 300 mm lens.

One of the most effective ways of using a telephoto to give a completely new perspective on everday subjects, subjects you might normally ignore is to exploit the narrow field of view to make highly selective compositions, picking out small details not readily apparent to the naked eye. By looking through a 300 mm lens, for instance, at a wide cityscape you can pick out unusual buildings and allow small sections of them to fill the frame. Try using the lens to compare old buildings with the new, or to create abstract compositions out of modern architectural designs. 500 mm mirror lenses are a particular favourite with some photographers, for with their narrow angle of view, flat perspective and almost total lack of depth of field, they can act almost like scissors—snipping out parts of the world around you. This can enable you to transform a scene into flat blocks of colour, tone and texture, isolating shapes and patterns and taking away any sense of form from three-dimensional objects.

In landscape photography the ability to be able to pick out details from a sweeping view is a valuable attribute. For this reason, many landscape photographers are found more often with a 200 or 300 mm lens than with a wide angle. These telephotos can allow you to pick out particularly attractive features of the landscape—patterned fields, shapely trees or perhaps a distant farm building to give a sense of scale to a wider area. On a more practical note, long telephotos allow you to reach well beyond, for example, a boring foreground and to concentrate on the main area of interest.

Associated with this selectivity is a telephoto's ability to create striking juxtapositions. A small foreground object, for instance, can be made to appear the same size as a huge building in the background. Similarly, two totally incompatible subjects can be made to relate to one another in terms of spatial positioning. For instance, a yacht sailing on the lake in a city park can appear to be floating on the very doorsteps of skyscrapers up in the background.

This ability to juxtapose unusual subjects is also an ideal way of bringing colour to a fairly monochrome scene. With a 300 or 400 mm lens you might try photographing a landscape or cityscape but shooting through a colourful row of flowers, defocused in the foreground. Alternatively, the foreground could be made a sharp and important element of a scene. An illuminated street lamp or traffic light could be composed against a background of an office building. If you choose your viewpoint with care and stop the lens down all the way, both elements will be sharp and the juxtapositions can be striking.

Another way long telephotos can be used creatively is to exploit the extremely shallow depth of field that these lenses have. By shooting at wide apertures, the background will be rendered an indistinct blur while the

Bagged fish *A long lens is ideal for picking out and emphasizing a detail that might otherwise go unnoticed—like the bag in the boy's hand*

main subject is given prominence since it has been lifted away from its surroundings. This feature of long lenses is a great advantage with subjects like sport—for instance, a tennis player can be isolated from the background.

Once you start experimenting with lenses of extremely long focal length— say an 800 mm or even 1000 mm or more— the creative possibilities are unlimited. Huge suns or moons can be composed in

Giraffe café *The compression of these lenses can create juxtapositions and distorted comparisons of scale that are not apparent to the naked eye*

Spiral staircase *A long telephoto encourages the observation of small details and allows them to be made into strong graphic images*

Anchor *Sometimes a detail is more striking than an overall view, but for close-ups of large subjects a long telephoto is essential*

Bjorn Borg *Lenses of this type are also indispensible for sport, allowing the photographer to fill the frame and eliminate distracting backgrounds*

a frame or photographed in conjunction with an ordinary scene—perhaps using the extreme telephoto for one exposure and making a second exposure on the same frame with a lens of more modest focal length. The total lack of depth can also be used creatively for strong graphic designs carefully framed by scanning your surroundings through the viewfinder and picking out shapes that could otherwise pass unnoticed.

While exciting pictures can be made in this random approach—sweeping your surroundings and looking through

the viewfinder at the shapes that appear—most strong telephoto images are created by the photographer's awareness of what makes a particularly good subject for the lens. For instance, the foreshortening effect can be exploited to emphasize the curves in a winding road while the tunnelling effect of an arched wooded gladed can be further exaggerated. Rows of cars held up in traffic, or of lamps lining a busy motorway are both similar subjects which can often be used to create dynamic images using a long telephoto.

Telephotos longer than 200 mm undeniably have great creative potential and can allow you to create exciting and unusual photographs—simply because they 'see' things in a totally different way to the human eye. However, in order not to be disappointed with the results, remember that using long lenses entails various technical problems, not the least or which is camera shake and mirror vibration. To get the most out of your long telephoto shots, you will need to get into the habit of using a tripod at all times and using your camera's mirror lock facility, where fitted. The unusual optical characteristics of these lenses will only have impact if your final prints or transparencies are perfectly sharp.

Mountain lion *The magnifying effect has an obvious application in wildlife photography where the subject is often some distance away*

Water skier *Getting close to the subject helps create impact but it is also essential to look for dynamic or interesting shapes in the frame*

Construction *Here the compressed perspective helped lead the eye to the construction worker and made the rods a feature rather than a distraction*

Chapter 2
COLOUR, GRAIN AND CONTRAST
Grain and contrast

The usual aim of a photographer is to produce pictures that are grain-free and which avoid extremes of contrast. Sometimes, however, obvious graininess and either very high or low contrast can actually be advantageous, and offer a new creative element to bring out the mood or style of a photograph.

Although it is possible to decide how to treat a photograph in the darkroom, or to go through your files for images that are suitable for a particular treatment, it is best to take pictures specifically with the effects you have in mind, on the most appropriate materials. Then not only are you technically prepared, you are also mentally geared up to seeing each scene as it will appear in the final picture, often radically changed.

The difference between black and white and colour is much more marked when you are trying for these effects. A low contrast, grainy image may look dreamlike and romantic in colour, but merely flat and boring in black and white. And a high contrast black and white image can appear striking, while in colour the strong hues may appear garish and disconcerting.

Some of the most appealing and easily produced results are those which are

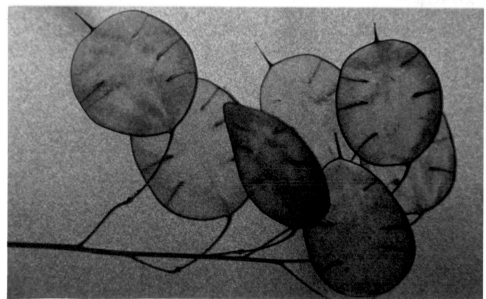

very grainy. In black and white this is easy enough to achieve by using a very fast film with almost any subject. However, when contrast is greatly increased, such as by using high contrast 'lith' film, you will have to select subjects more carefully. Similarly, if you were planning to make very large

Landscape *Pin sharp resolution of detail is not always essential for landscape work— here fast film gave a grainy effect while the contrast of the light separated the foreground from the background.* **Seed pods** *An exaggerated grainy effect can also be created by using texture screens during the duplicating process*

sectional enlargments to exploit a film's graininess, you should choose your film with great care—not too fine a grain, and not too contrasty, such as 2475 recording film, or uprate a normal fast film. Alternatively you could enlarge a small section of the film, though this demands a good quality enlarger lens and maybe very long exposures. Generally it is best to aim for the highest acutance and sharpness and the least clumped-together grain.

Grain alone can play a major role in the impact of a photograph. For example, in black and white, where the print is already an abstraction from reality, large and obvious grain accentuates this abstraction. The mood of the picture becomes stark and uncompromising, more graphic and heavy. It goes well with emotional, depressing or gloomy subjects—a weary work-lined face, a densely packed cemetery or an ugly industrial scene. Graininess adds to the coarse feel of these subjects, expressing the photographic equivalent of roughness. It can also emphasize drama since it rides roughshod over subtle mid tones. Smooth tonal variations are transformed into harder, sudden changes from light to dark, and details are obscured. Your attention becomes focused on shapes and masses, like the shape of a tree rather than its constituent leaves and branches: or the massiveness of a factory, rather than its windows.

While graininess is most commonly used for high contrast subjects, it can be used with low contrast scenes as well, such as misty views, particularly if you take great care to keep not only the image but the individual grains sharp.

Field patterns *Striking graphic effects can be produced by isolating a few contrasting patches of landscape—like these sections of fields.*

Solitary house *The grain of fast black and white film is ideal for conveying the bleakness in scenes like this. Hard paper brought out all the subtle contrast variations.*

Dancer *Deliberately opting for a minimum of contrast also suits certain subjects—especially when trying to establish a soft, romantic mood.*

Window shutter *Extreme grain can be achieved by enlarging a small portion of the original 35 mm slide on to 5 × 4 in. film*

Then each particle is seen as a tiny black dot, and the image visibly breaks up into what seems to be individual particles. A view of a smog filled street would work very well in this way—it would seem as if you were looking at the smoke and dust motes themselves.

Such low contrast black and white images work best with subjects which have naturally low contrast, as with mist. The result is unreal and intangible, and the grain tends to reinforce this appearance, as you can see that the image consists of nothing but a mass of insubstantial dots. So if you want to exploit the method you should take original pictures which are high key, with very little range of brightness in them. One area of experimentation, for example, would be to make someone appear almost wraithlike, consisting solely of a collection of specks of matter. Do this by photographing the subject on grainy film against a light background on an overcast day. Make sure that there is very little difference in brightness in the scene—dress the subject in light coloured clothes with only a small difference in tone between them and the background. Then make a light, low contrast print, so that there are no tones in the background at all. Some dodging may be needed to get the right effect.

You can also look around for subjects which will turn simply into a mass of tones when given the grainy treatment. The results may be completely abstract, in which case you must take care that the final picture retains some point. An example might be the interplay of shadows across a surface: the picture would be meaningless unless you included a recognizable shadow.

Once you turn to colour, the situation changes completely. Those subjects that become dramatic or striking with prominent grain in black and white, such as city streets, can appear merely carelessly or crudely photographed in colour. But grainy colour pictures have their own appeal, whether the colours are bright or subtle.

There are a number of methods of getting grainy results in colour. The simplest is to use grainy material to start with. One film, now discontinued, that was very popular for this purpose was GAF 500, an ISO 500 film—quite grainy by current colour film emulsion standards. But with modern film you can enlarge the images taken on fast films to emphasize the grain: some photographers deliberately use 110 format for exactly this reason, but even then some considerable enlargement is needed. Pictures taken in such a way have a quite different appearance from those which are on uprated film, as the dyed grains themselves become visible. The effect is very like the *pointilliste* technique of Impressionist painting, which sought to reproduce colours in an additive way by using dots of different colours. In the case of a photograph, the grains are cyan, magenta and yellow.

Industrial scene *Black and white film is well suited to recording tonal extremes—here the brooding ominous sky contrasts with the buildings*

You can enlarge transparencies directly on to film, if you wish, by using your camera without the lens under the enlarger or projector. The graininess of the copy film will have little effect on the graininess of the result, but your choice of copy film allows you to get either high contrast images, by copying on to a slow film such as Kodachrome, or low contrast ones, by using duplicating, or fast, film.

High contrast grainy images inevitably mean strong colour saturation, with vivid hues. Take pictures with this in mind, remembering that you may be using only part of the image, and that this part should be very sharp. Strongly coloured objects, blue skies and bright sunshine are needed. You should also aim for very simple, graphic images. Some subjects which are not quite ideal for an ordinary shot might work well with the grainy treatment—small blemishes in the paintwork of an object could become submerged in the grain, or the colour of a slightly faded article could be exaggerated.

The bright, simple images produced by these techniques can be applied to a wide variety of subjects—flowers, bright paintwork—any brightly coloured scene has potential. What the effects all have in common is that the results are no longer representations of the subject—they have turned into images. The viewer cannot ignore the fact that they are images, made of dyes on film or paper, and are not made to look like faithful copies of the original.

Grainy results are also popular for low contrast images. Some photographers, such as David Hamilton, specialize in these soft, romantic, dreamy pictures. But there is a considerable difference between these grainy images and soft focus, which is produced by other methods (see pages 66 to 69). Soft focus tends to give rather mushy results, while low contrast grainy images appear

almost painterly in quality. In these pictures, harsh lighting and bright colours are usually avoided, as the aim is to produce photographs which look as if they belong to a bygone era.

Flowers and landscapes are also suited to this approach, though again the lighting should be diffuse or mellow. Having experimented with graininess, it is also possible to alter the contrast of a subject in its own right, without aiming for grainy results. In the case of black and white, the traditional way of increasing contrast is to copy on to high contrast film, but you can also use slow, contrasty film in the camera. Microfilm is particularly suitable for this.

Moderately high contrast has a documentary quality, since news pictures are frequently copied and recopied, particularly archive material. You can lend an air of immediacy to some otherwise mundane scenes by this technique.

In colour, high contrast can be achieved by successively duplicating an image. It can produce vivid images from those which previously lacked strong colour, but the originals must be chosen with care. Those with areas of uniform colour, and with little overall brightness range, will work best. Flesh tones can take on an unattractive cast, appearing orange or brown.

Banana Even in the studio, deliberate exaggeration of grain can produce striking results, and is effective especially with bold shapes and strong colours

Cityscapes Here, dramatic contrast has been used to make the bright, sunlit office block stand out strongly from the dark, shadowed foreground

Bridge The grainy appearance of high speed colour transparency film has been exploited to underline the gloominess of this wet, foggy scene

Colour contrast

In the early days of colour photography, when colours could only be rendered in pale and muted hues, photographers naturally tended to select subjects suited to a pastel look. With modern emulsions, however, colours can be bright and fully saturated and the handling of colour in photographs has developed accordingly. Just like other visual artists such as painters and interior designers, photographers have begun to explore the creative potential of strong, contrasting colours.

Reactions to different colours seems to vary so much from person to person that it seems colour response is largely subjective—perhaps this is because so little is known about human colour vision. Yet there is no doubt that most people find strong colours more stimulating than weak colours, if not necessarily more pleasing—bright red even sounds more exciting than pale red. Naturally, then, a photograph containing strong, bright colours tends to provoke a more positive response than one in which the colours are generally pale. At the simplest level, this means that it is often worth including a splash of colour (preferably red) in the frame to 'lift' the picture. But there is no reason why you should not go much further and make strong colour the dominant element.

Strongly coloured pictures are not necessarily completely satisfying—that depends on the way the colour is used— but they can often be immediately attractive, which is why so many advertisements use them. They catch the eye and provoke a definite response, whether it is of like or dislike.

Of course, there is no shortage of potential subjects. To the generally soft hues of nature, have been added the colours made possible by modern paints, dyes and plastics. Bright colours —once the preserve of flowers—are now to be found everywhere. City centres in particular are often a riot of colour. Indeed, bright colours have become so commonplace that it is easy to pass them by without noticing—and this is the photographer's chance. You can move in and isolate them with the camera, to bring them back into view and show what a colourful place the city can be. Or, by selective framing, you can use the areas of bright colour in much the same way that the artist uses paint, and create almost abstract images.

The beauty is that virtually any brightly coloured object can be turned to creative use. By closing in and isolating it from its surroundings you can treat it in such a way that the colour is highlighted and its function becomes all but irrelevant-the yellow dustbin is no longer a dustbin but part of a design in yellow.

Simplicity is the essence of these pictures. Too much fussy detail ruins the effect. Concentrate on small uncluttered areas and aim to include just one or two strong colours in the frame—any more tends to confuse the eye and actually reduces the impression of brightness in the image.

However, it is not always enough to merely frame an area of bright colour: you should try to manipulate it to create a photograph. It is easy to be beguiled by the attractiveness of strong colour into thinking that once you have isolated the colour in the viewfinder, you have done enough. But the effect soon palls.

Look for blocks of colour, lines, shadows, texture and other details and use the frame to arrange them into a design. If there is a strong line across the surface of your subject, for instance, use it positively to enhance the mood. With an abstract approach, there is no reason why the camera should be held level— an unusual angle giving strong diagonal

Yellow field *Exploiting colour contrast can be an effective way of taking landscapes with a difference. Keep the image extremely simple and use the frame to 'design' the picture—note how the cloud echoes the wood*

Balconies *Although colours in the shade are generally dull, a subtle contrast can make the shot interesting*

lines can often help to accentuate the vibrant, energetic effect of strong colour.

Alternatively, look for small, interesting details to act as a focal point—there is no need for the picture to be completely abstract.

For these strong colour shots to have their full impact, of course, they must be bright and well saturated. The diffuse lighting of a dull day is often recommended for full colour saturation, but this only really works well for soft, subtle hues; strong colours tend to lose some of their brightness in dull, cloudy weather. So although saturation may actually be less, it is better to wait for strong sunshine. Indeed it seems that the more light there is, the better, for this kind of shot. Beaches and coastal resorts where strong sun is reflected from the sea, and modern cities where white concrete and glass surfaces throw light everywhere, are undoubtedly among the best places to work—and, of course, there is usually plenty of subject matter available.

Red band *Strong colour can give even the most mundane object potential for striking abstracts. Remember to use lines and blocks of colour—like the broad red band sweeping from corner to corner in this shot—to create a complete picture*

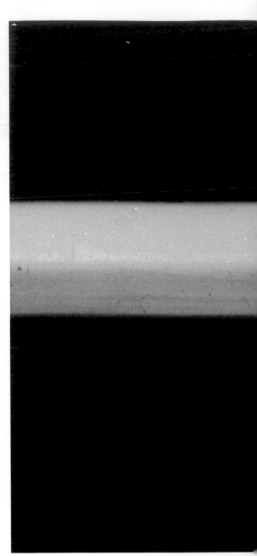

Making a point *A pure black makes an effective background for any brightly coloured subject*

Blue corner *An unusual view of a familiar sight, the corner of a pool —strong diagonals enhance the high energy feel of colour contrast pictures*

One problem is that in strong sunlight it is easy to overexpose shots, giving pale, washed out colours. It is important, therefore, to underexpose slide film— perhaps up to full two stops—to give colours their full value.

But perhaps the most interesting way of giving colours their full impact is to exploit colour contrast. It has been firmly established by psychologists that our judgement of the brightness of a colour is strongly influenced by the surrounding colours. If you look at two identical squares, one with a black border and the other with a white, the square surrounded by black will seem much brighter than the white edged square. In contrast to the black border, the square seems very bright to the eye:

next to the white border it does not. So whenever there is a dark tone—light tone border, the dark tone seems darker and the light tone brighter than it actually is.

Contrasting colours are essentially colours opposite each other on the traditional colour circle—that is, complementary colours such as blue and yellow, red and cyan, and green and magenta. A colour will appear to be much brighter next to its complementary than next to any other colour. And even when the adjacent colour is not complementary, the eye tends to see it as if it is.

You can exploit the way the eye reacts to colour contrast to give strong colour pictures an added vibrancy—and also to increase the impact of many other shots. So when out looking for strong colour shots look for colour contrasts in particular—wherever there is a good colour contrast, there is

potential for a shot.

Because of the tendency of the eye to maximise the differences between colours, the colours need not be complementary for an effective contrast. Indeed, one of the most effective contrasts is between red and blue. Because red 'advances' in a picture and blue 'recedes', the difference between them can be so marked that a picture that is just pure red and pure blue seems to positively vibrate. So for a vibrant, high energy effect, you could look for a low viewpoint of bright red objects to contrast them against a piercing blue sky. To enhance the effect, use a polarizing filter to deepen the blue of the sky.

Although blue and red provide the most striking contrasts, many other combinations, both subtle and strong can be very effective. But it is important that the boundaries between the colours are very marked—soft edges reduce the effect of the contrast. This is why man-made environments often have more potential than nature. Colours should also be fairly pure—gradations of colour similarly tend to reduce the effect. So places where strong sunshine flattens colours and where there are plenty of large, simple shapes are the best

Doorway An array of colours as
varied as this rarely works though
here the simple, angular shapes help
make a successful shot
Three trees In late spring, arable farming
land is filled with brightly-coloured crops,
like rape, that contrast well with blue sky

hunting grounds—again modern cities and also beaches and deserts are the places to look.

While strong colour contrast is ideal for striking abstract and surreal images, you can also use it in many other contexts to enliven an image. It can help, for instance, to choose the colour of your background by looking for a contrasting colour.

In the studio, for instance, you can use a cold blue background to contrast

Sliding doors *Look out for bright reds. Colour film is particularly good at rendering them accurately*

Hang glider *The strongest colour contrasts are between complementary colours such as orange and blue.*
Yellow roof *For bright, well saturated colours, shoot in strong sunlight and underexpose by a few stops*

with warm skin tones—advertisers often use a blue background to give an extra glow to the amber of a glass of whisky lit from underneath. But whatever you choose to do, remember that colour appreciation is largely subjective—a colour combination that seems attractive to you may be stomach churning for someone else.

Rice harvest *In scenes with mostly natural colours—browns and greens —look for some red to enliven the shot*
Big wheel *Set a bright red subject against a clear blue sky and use a polarizing filter to make it richer*

Chapter 3
COLOUR EFFECTS
Flash colour

Coloured filters are a very effective way of changing the colour of a photograph to achieve a desired effect. Unfortunately, when used on the camera, they filter the whole image and colour areas you may want to retain in their natural hues. But there is no reason why you should not put filters over an ordinary flashgun and direct it to colour just part of the subject. And by using several filtered flashguns together you can illuminate various areas in different coloured light to produce a brightly coloured picture from even the drabbest subject.

Even when you want to create a naturalistic look, it is often a good idea to filter the light from your flashgun—this can warm up the picture to give it a cosy glow, or compensate for colour in a ceiling from which you want to bounce the flash light.

Colouring the background
One of the simplest ways to use filtered flash is to colour the background while maintaining natural colour in the foreground. You could, for instance, use filtered flash to give an outdoor shot a deep blue background by loading your camera with tungsten-balanced colour slide film, and fitting a suitable orange filter over your flashgun.

The effect works by exploiting the tendency of tungsten light balanced colour film to give very blue results in daylight. If you use the filtered flash to illuminate the subject, only the background will have this very blue colour while the subject will be rendered in warm, natural colours.

This technique works best on an overcast day, or when the sky is blue and the sun obscured by clouds. Under these conditions, the light has a high blue content, and is not as bright as when the sun is shining, making it easier to balance the natural light with that of the electronic flash.

Choose a film with a fairly slow speed, such as ISO 64 or 100, so that you can use the slow shutter speed necessary for flash synchronization without overexposing the background. The filter over the flashgun should be an orange 85B or its equivalent. Since the filter is not used over the camera lens, it need not be optically perfect, and you can use acrylic lighting gel. These are widely used in the film industry, and are available from theatrical lighting suppliers.

They are made in a great variety of colours, but the best for this type of shot is a full orange gel, which converts light from a colour temperature of 5500 to approximately 3200K.

The exposure is made by both flashlight and daylight and these must be carefully balanced. Start by consulting the exposure table on your flashgun. If this is an automatic model, select an aperture of f/5.6 or f/8, and set this on the lens. Then take a meter reading to determine the correct shutter speed. Make sure that the shutter speed is slow enough to synchronize with the flash. If it is not, use the next smaller aperture offered by your flashgun.

By setting the shutter speed and aperture in this manner, you are assuming that the flash and daylight exposures are being made independently. Since they are not, and both are contributing to the overall exposure, you must close the aperture down by one stop, or the foreground will be overexposed. Finally, make a few bracketing exposures, changing the aperture setting one stop either way—if you change the shutter speed to bracket the photographs, the intensity of the foreground illumination remains constant, and only the brightness of the daylight-lit background changes (though you can use this to control the appearance of the picture).

With a manual flash, you must compensate for the light absorption of the orange filter—this means using an aperture two thirds of a stop wider than that recommended by the calculator dial or table.

Filter swatch *Acrylic lighting gels come in a staggering variety of shades and hues. They can be used on a flash, but not over the lens*

Alternative colours

If you want a background colour other than blue, a different technique is required to achieve it. To do this you must use a filter over both the lens and the flashgun. If the two filters are of complementary colours, the foreground will appear on film in its normal hue, and the background will come out the colour of the filter over the lens. You can check if two filters are of complementary colours by holding them both up to the light. They should look a neutral grey colour when you look through both at once. If they look any other colour, the foreground will be tinted in this same hue when you use them to take pictures.

Filter pairs which are specially matched for this technique are widely available, but if you have brightly coloured filters for contrast control in – black and white photography, you could use these over the lens instead. Choose one that is the colour you want to tint the background, then go through a swatch of lighting gel filters until you find the complementary colour. Then tape a piece of this gell over your flash.

Deeply coloured filters can absorb a considerable amount of light—perhaps as much as four stops—so you must allow for this light loss when you calculate exposure. The TTL meter in your camera takes into account the daylight absorbed by the filter over the lens, but not that from the flash. The sensor in an automatic flashgun takes into account the light absorbed by the filter over the flash, but not by the filter over the lens. Unless the camera has off-the-film flash metering, you must compensate for the filter over the lens by setting a slower film speed on the calculator dial of your flashgun. The compensation needed depends on the density of the filter. You can measure this by taking TTL meter readings with and without the filter fitted to the lens. The difference between the two readings is the required compensation in stops. Once you have worked this out, and made the adjustment on the flashgun, you can determine exposure as before.

With a long time exposure, you can use this coloured background technique to make strange, surreal images with

Multicoloured model *The brilliant colours in the picture were produced using three flashguns, with the reflectors covered in red, green and blue lighting gels. Because these are the primary colours they produced white light where all three overlap, and yellow, cyan or magenta where the model obscured one of the guns. It is possible to produce the same effect with other colours, but beware of undesirable colour casts like the one in the picture directly above*

moving subjects, particularly if you take care to balance the daylight and flash-light exactly. The flash freezes the image of a moving object at one point in its path, and this sharp image appears naturally coloured. In addition, however, the time exposure catches a trail of the moving object, and this is rendered in the colour of the filter over the lens. As with all experimental techniques, you must be prepared for a little trial and error before you achieve successful results. So do not be disheartened if your first results are not perfect.

Additional flashguns
If you have access to more than one flashgun, you can use filtered flash to create even more special effects. Try using one gun to backlight your subject, with a strongly coloured filter over the reflector. This gun can be fired by a long extension cable or a slave cell, to form a halo of coloured light around the edge of the subject. Since it is only providing highlight illumination, it does not con-tribute much to the overall exposure, and providing it is not a particularly powerful unit, it can be ignored for the purposes of exposure calculations.

If you use two flashguns for front lighting, you can cover the reflectors with lighting gels in complementary colours. Where the scene is lit by both guns, the two colours combine to produce white light, and the subject appears in its natural shades. The shadow areas, on the other hand, are lit by only one gun, and they take on a colour cast which matches the colour of the filter over that flash.

In the same way, you can use three guns, and cover each with a filter in one of the three primary colours—red, green and blue—or their complemen-taries—cyan, magenta and yellow. Again, where the beams of light from all three flashes overlap, white light is produced, but in the shadows there is a colour cast. This is most clearly visible if the main subject is quite close to the background: if it is far away, the back-ground will appear as a solid black. For best results, set the flashguns at least half a metre apart, or the shadows look very small and tightly packed.

Whenever more than one light source is used, the exposure must be adjusted to take the extra light into account. If you use two automatic flashguns with filters on each, you should close the lens aperture to one stop smaller than that indicated on the guns themselves. With three guns, you should use 1½ stops compensation. If you are using manual guns, the absorption of light by the coloured filters must also be taken into account when calculating exposure.

A few of the more recent cameras, such as the Olympus OM2, the Pentax LX and the Nikon F3, measure flash directly from the film plane, and with these models, no compensation of any sort is needed—you can use them as if you are taking pictures with a single, unfiltered flash unit.

Filtering for realism
Besides filtering the light from your flash to produce an unreal effect, you can also use filters when you are aiming for very natural lighting. Bouncing light from a ceiling or wall is a very useful way of converting the harsh illumination of a flashgun to a more normal light, but coloured paintwork may give an un-pleasant colour cast to the subject. But as long as the paintwork is not too dark, a filter on the flashgun in a complemen-tary colour can compensate for the unwanted colour. If you do not have the exact shade of gel that you want, aim for one which is slightly too yellow, rather than too blue, as warm colours usually look more pleasing.

Neutral density filters can sometimes be used to cut down the power output of a flash, particularly when working at close range. Even the smallest flashgun often needs an aperture of $f/32$ if it is used for macro work, and many lenses cannot be stopped down this far. Using a ND filter over the lens is not always the answer, since this prevents you from using any available light to illuminate the background. Grey lighting gels on the flashgun cut back light on the subject only. These acrylic filters can be used many layers thick, and one large sheet of 0.3 ND filtration can provide upwards of one stop cut in flash output.

Automatic flashguns frequently have a minimum working distance, below which they produce overexposure. Used in a similar manner, grey gels can reduce this minimum distance considerably. They can also reduce the risk of reciprocity failure when using an auto-matic flashgun at short distances. Com-puter flash units control light output by cutting off the flash very rapidly when the subject is very close or pale in

Calculating exposure
If you are using a filter to colour the background, and a complementary coloured flash to light the foreground, you may have difficulty in figuring out how much exposure is needed. Follow this simple procedure to arrive at the correct settings.

1 First, use the TTL meter on your camera to measure the light absorbed by each filter. Do this by taking a meter reading with and without the filter in place on the lens. The difference between the readings, measured in stops, with and without the filter gives the filter factor in each case.

2 Now consult the chart or dial on your flashgun to find the working aperture. For a manual flashgun you must take into account the light absorbed by the filter over the reflector—you measured this at step 1—but a computer gun com-pensates automatically.

3 Set this initial f-stop on the camera lens, and then open up the aperture enough to compensate for the light absorbed by the filter over the camera lens.

4 Finally, take a TTL meter reading in the normal way to work out the correct shutter speed for the aperture.
Remember that the shutter speed you use must be slow enough to synchronize with the flashgun. This generally means a speed slower than 1/60 or 1/125.

colour. The very brief flash that results cause a colour shift, but by taping ND filters over the flashgun, the duration of the flash is increased, and colour rendering returns to normal.

Balancing act *Several flashguns can be used in combination, by fixing them to a ruler or a piece of timber*

Polarized colour

Many pictures can be ruined by the glaring *polarized* light reflected from shiny surfaces such as plate glass and water. Polarizing filters reduce or remove this, without substantially affecting the colour balance of the shot. They can also be used to darken a blue sky to give the shot more impact.

There are, however, a number of other creative techniques you can use to control the effect of the polarizing filter on each shot. By adjusting the filter on the lens, you can cut out varying degrees of the sheen or gloss given off by highly reflective surfaces, which 'dilutes' colours and can mask texture. Some shiny, polished surfaces give off strong, specular reflections, and these can be almost entirely suppressed by the polarizer.

In landscapes, haze can weaken colour, especially on the horizon on sunny days. While this is sometimes desirable for certain effects, when not needed it can be reduced by the polarizing filter, giving better colour.

Polarizer technique

The best way to judge the effect the filter will have on your shot is to look directly through the filter itself, either through the viewfinder of an SLR

Sky and bus *Light from a blue sky is strongly polarized and you can use a polarizing filter to deepen its colour if you are at 90° to the sun*

Brilliant bridge *A vari-colour polarizing filter can be used for dramatic colour changes simply by turning a ring*

camera or by holding it up to your eye.

Rotating the filter has the effect of cutting out light polarized in different planes. When the plane of this polarized light is at 90 degrees to the filter's plane of polarization, the filter's effect is greatest—it cuts out the maximum amount of polarized light. This is useful when, for example, you want to darken the sky in a shot. Most polarizers have a mark on the rim, and when this mark is lined up to point at the sun, the filter's plane of polarization is at 90 degrees to the plane of polarization of the light from the sun. The sky is thus darkened as much as possible.

However, since light in any given scene is polarized in many planes and it is not always possible to work out what these are, you can get the surest idea by looking through the filter itself. Rotate the filter until you obtain the effect you want, bearing in mind that there is no point in rotating it more than 180 degrees, since the range of effects is repeated every half turn.

Leaf and car *Vari-colour polarizers affect polarized light differentially. Here, the colour of the car windscreen has been changed by rotating the filter*

Brightening colours

Glossy non-metallic surfaces give off polarized light, which is not the colour of the surfaces themselves but the colour of the incident light, usually white or bluish white. This effect obscures the real colour of the surface which will not appear saturated or bright when photographed. All but completely rough or matt surfaces reflect some polarized light, but it is normally only a problem with shiny surfaces such as leaves, paint, pavements in the rain, polished surfaces, leather and skin. By rotating the polarizer to cut out as much as possible of this sheen, you can render the true colour of your subject much

more clearly and brilliantly and perhaps avoid unpleasant burnt out highlights. Professionals, for example, use a polarizing filter when photographing furniture, to show the grain of the wood more clearly. Be careful not to overdo correction, though, for some subjects need the sheen to retain their original sparkle.

Reflections

Sheen is usually diffused and subdued —reflections are much more noticeable, and can be very undesirable in certain shots. Polished paintwork, plastic, glass and water all give off strong reflections which may hide their colours almost completely. Such reflections can be reduced or even removed by a polarizing filter, but it cannot suppress the reflections in mirrors or polished metals such as chrome.

The effectiveness of a polarizer at suppressing reflections depends on the angle of the lens relative to the reflecting surface, and what this surface is composed of. Every shiny substance has an

optimum angle, and if light is reflected off its surface at this angle, the reflected beam is completely polarized. This has a number of practical implications.

If you are trying to completely remove reflections from a shop window, or from a still pool of water, for instance, it means that you must point your camera at the surface at a very precise angle. For water, this angle is 53°; for plate glass, it is 56°. If your lens is pointed at the surface at this optimum angle, and the polarizer rotated carefully, every trace of the reflection disappears in the centre of the field of view. At the edges, where the angle of the reflected light is slightly different, elimination of reflections is not so complete, but usually this is noticeable only with wide angle lenses.

Although the angle between lens and surface is critical, it does not need to be accurately measured. Simply by looking through the viewfinder and moving the camera back and forth, you should soon pick out the best angle at which to aim

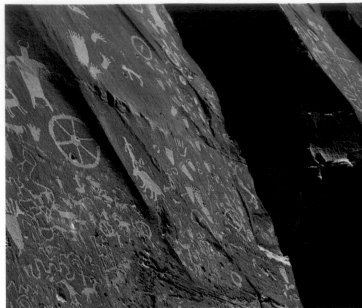

the lens.

Since a polarizing filter is only effective within quite a narrow range of angles, roughly at a diagonal to the reflecting surface, its usefulness is limited. If the camera is being pointed directly at a window, for example, there is no point in using one, as its ability to cut reflections is negligible.

If you are photographing moving water or a rough sea, a polarizer is not very useful either, because the water surface is constantly being broken up by waves. With still or gently rippling water, however, a polarizer can totally remove reflections.

When cutting out reflections from polished surfaces, watch out for stress marks which show as coloured areas. Windscreens show bands of colour, and some plastics show marks which are not visible when they are photographed normally.

Darkening the sky

Polarizing filters can be used to darken the sky, on bright, sunny days when the sky produces large amounts of polarized light. In some colour shots without a polarizer, the sky can appear to be almost white, rather than blue, but when a polarizer is used this effect is greatly reduced and skies can be very deep blue.

The amount of polarized light in the sky varies according to the angle of the sun. Areas at right-angles to the sun contain the most, so the filter has its greatest effect when the view is at right-angles to the sun. The final result therefore depends on the season and the latitude as well as on the direction in which the camera is aimed. When the sun is high, the filter affects the area of sky nearest the horizon—when the sun is low, on the other hand, the areas of sky overhead are darkened most.

With a wide angle lens, however, you may easily include areas of sky with

Uneven sky *With a polarizer and a wide angle lens, the sky may appear on film as a patchy, uneven shade of blue*

differently polarized light. Consequently the filter's effect is not uniform across the whole picture area, and the result is often visibly artificial and far from pleasing.

Normally you will find that the filter setting which darkens the sky most also removes other unwanted effects such as sheen or reflections from the ground or water, and a single setting provides all the effects you want.

Haze

Light scattered by dust and moisture in the atmosphere, causing haze, contains a proportion of polarized light. This haze can sometimes be reduced by a polarizing filter, allowing you to bring out elements in a landscape which would otherwise be lost. Again, do not be indiscriminate in using the filter, but consider whether the landscape really benefits by the inclusion of the haze.

When there is just a slight haze in the distance rather than a definite mist, try using a polarizer and a UV or haze filter

Cave paintings *Unwanted reflections from very shiny surfaces can be removed very effectively with a polarizing filter*

together. Because it cuts out some of the stray light which causes distant haze, the filter brightens up the colours of the scene generally. No polarizer alone can completely elminate haze of this kind, as it does not have much effect on the long range blue rays cut out by the haze filter. Some polarizers, however, have their own UV/haze cutting elements built in. Exposure can be long with this set-up, because the filter factor is considerable, so you might try using a tripod to avoid camera shake.

Exposure

Because a polarizer cuts out some light rays, it has much the same effect as a neutral density filter, and so you must increase the exposure by about one and a half to two stops.

With most cameras incorporating TTL meters, calculating the extra exposure is no problem but some cameras incorporate beam splitters in their exposure meters. When these are used with a normal polarizing filter, they may give totally wrong readings because the beam splitter reflects light partially, and polarizes it at the same time, blacking out or boosting the reading.

With this type of camera, use a circular polarizer. This filter has one component which acts in the same way as a normal polarizer, but also includes another sheet which gives the light rays a 'twist' as they leave the filter, so that instead of vibrating in just one plane they travel in a spiral. They then pass through the beamsplitter without giving a false reading.

With slow films, long exposure times are almost certainly necessary with all but the brightest subjects. If you plan to do a great deal of work with slow colour films, you would do well to invest in the best quality polarizer you can find. It might gain a whole stop more than you would get from a cheap one.

Additionally, high quality polarizing filters absorb all colours of polarized light equally, but you may find that a cheap filter does not. In practical terms, this means that instead of eliminating the reflection of the sun on a pool of water, you merely colour the reflected image a deep shade of purple. An inexpensive filter may, therefore, be a false economy.

Special techniques

Two polarizers combined, rotated independently of one another, act as a neutral density filter which can vary from ND 0.9 (which is dense) to nearly clear. When they are rotated to darker settings, they often produce a strong blue colour cast.

Colour polarizers are available which turn the different polarizations of light

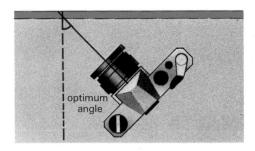

Critical angle *For best results, move around until the polarizer is at the correct angle to the reflecting surface*

into different colours. For example, a red–blue colour polarizer such as the Hoya vari-colour looks purple in appearance. Light passing through it polarized in one plane emerges coloured blue, while light polarized at 90° to it comes out as red. Unpolarized light comes out purple.

A colour polarizer combined with a normal polarizer produces a variable colour filter. These are normally made to give a single colour filter with continuously variable density.

By combining a two colour polarizer such as the red–blue mentioned above, with a plain polarizer, you produce a filter which has variable colour instead of variable density.

Although polarizing filters are only effective when light is reflected from the subject at one specific angle, there is a technique that can be used in the studio to totally eliminate reflections, whatever the relative position of surface and camera.

This is to use polarizing material over both the light source and the lens. This

Shop window *If the camera is pointed directly at a reflective surface, reflections are inevitable, even with a polarizer. By carefully choosing your viewpoint, however, you can eliminate reflections almost entirely*

system is ideal for irregular, highly reflective subjects such as varnished oil paintings.

Large sheets of polarizing material are stretched over the light sources so that all the light that falls on the subject is polarized in the same plane. If the lights are hot, as is the case with tungsten lighting, or studio flash with modelling lights, special heatproof material must be used.

Light which falls on rough parts of the subject becomes depolarized, and passes straight through the polarizing filter on the lens, but light reflected from shiny surfaces retains its polarization, and is stopped by the filter on the lens.

Polarized darkground is a method used for close-up pictures through bellows or microscopes, with subjects which rotate or change the orientation of polarized light passing through them (such as crystals and plastics of many kinds). One polarizer is placed between the light source and the illuminated subject, and another between the subject and the camera. Correctly aligned, the subject shows up in bright colours on a bright background. With a colour polarizer in place in place of the filter below the subject, you can produce a coloured background.

For unusual and striking results, you can try placing a sheet of flat polarizing material over a lamp. Aiming the camera, fitted with a polarizing filter, vertically down, place any piece of cellophane or clear plastic, such as a cigarette wrapper, on the flat polarizing sheet. By rotating the filter on the lens, you can achieve a wide range of coloured effects.

With certain types of plastic, the coloured patterns are changed when the material is under stress. By holding a piece of clear acrylic sheet in front of the lens, and gently flexing it, the changes are clearly visible. This method is used for industrial stress testing.

Infrared colour

One of the most popular of all specialist films is infrared film. With its extra sensitivity to invisible infrared 'light', it has many scientific and technical uses, while its unusual colour and tone rendering give the creative photo-grapher tremendous scope. It is very simple to use and calls for little special equipment—it can be loaded into an ordinary SLR—but to get the best from infrared, you must follow a number of simple rules.

Infrared film is marketed by Kodak in black and white and colour slide versions and is available at many large photographic dealers. Both black and white and colour versions are similar in that they are sensitive to both infrared and visible light and in certain instances results on either can look similar to those on normal film. Nevertheless, each must be handled in a particular way because of their unique qualities.

Colour infrared
Ektachrome infrared, the colour infrared film, is sold in ordinary 35 mm film cassettes and can be loaded and un-loaded in subdued light in the same way as normal colour film. However, it must be stored in a freezer (but allowed time to warm up before use) and processed immediately after exposure. Poorly stored, the emulsion layers in the film age differently and the colour balance becomes biased towards cyan. Though you may be able to use this colour shift creatively, it is usually undesirable.

Like normal colour film, Ektachrome infrared has three emulsion layers each sensitive to a different primary colour. However, unlike conventional film, no

attempt is made to reproduce lifelike colours in the transparency. Green light forms a blue image, for example, and red light, a yellow one.

However, whenever there is any infrared present, as there is in most scenes, colours in the photograph begin to look much stranger. The film is particularly sensitive to the infrared reflected by healthy foliage—infrared film was originally designed to show up camouflage in World War 2—and foliage reproduces as bright red or magenta. Even the extra infrared reflected by blood makes veins just under the skin show up as brown lines in the slide.

Any blue in the subject will also distort colours and for technical pictures in daylight, where the aim is normally to show up areas of infrared reflection, you should put a Wratten 12 yellow filter on the camera to cut out the blue. For creative pictures, of course, this is not so important, but results are generally more attractive if you use a yellow filter. In tungsten lighting, for correct colour balance—that is, the balance the film is designed to give, which is by no means normal—you should use a CC 50 cyan filter as well.

When you are deliberately trying to introduce weird colours, you can experiment with any coloured filter on the camera to produce the desired effect—though the results are generally difficult to predict. For example, a yellow Wratten 8 filter produces a bluer cast to

Misty woods *With infrared film, a special focusing adjustment must b made, or pictures will be unsharp*

vegetation, a Wratten 21 a more orange cast, while a 25 red, among other things, usually gives a yellow sky.

Exposure for infrared film is not as simple as it is for conventional emulsions, simply because exposure meters are specifically designed to be sensitive only to the visible part of the spectrum. However, the amount of infrared radiation present out doors on any day is generally proportional to the level of visible light—when the sun shines, both infrared and visible light get brighter. So you can generally use the meter reading as a basis for calculating exposure. But since colour infrared is rated to include the reduction in light produced by the Wratten 12 yellow filter, a TTL meter reading with the filter in place indicates the wrong exposure. To estimate the correct exposure with a TTL meter set the film speed to 100 ASA (ISO), and take readings without a filter on the lens.

Readings taken on this basis should be appropriate for pictures taken through a Wratten 12 yellow filter, but with other filters, you need to give extra exposure. Filter factors are hard to estimate, because the characteristics of the filter may affect the infrared sensitive layer to a greater or lesser extent than the other layers. The only way to be certain of perfect exposure is to bracket the pictures at half or one stop intervals, for two stops on either side of the indicated exposure.

Ektachrome Infrared is processed by the obsolescent E4 system, which has been largely phased out. A few laboratories still process E4 films however, and you should contact Kodak for the address of your nearest lab.

Black and white
Kodak's infrared sensitive black and white film is called *High Speed Infrared*, and is available in 20 exposure cassettes of 35 mm film, and also as sheet film.

Like Ektachrome Infrared, it is sensitive to visible light as well as infrared, and when used with red filtration, it sometimes produces pictures which look fairly similar to those taken on ordinary black and white film.

However, High Speed Infrared is much more sensitive to infrared than Ektachrome and its extreme sensitivity means that it must be handled with great care. It is very susceptible to fogging by ambient infrared, and it must be loaded into the camera and unloaded in total darkness. The velvet light trap of the 35 mm cassette is transparent to infrared, and in direct sunlight, even the fabric of a changing bag may not prevent fogging. Load your camera in the darkroom before going out to take pictures, and if you have to reload during a session, do so with the camera and film in a changing bag in deep shade—ideally indoors.

Even your camera may be slightly transparent to infrared radiation, particularly any plastic components. Rangefinder cameras which have fabric focal plane shutters are especially susceptible to fogging of the film. Fortunately, in an SLR the infrared radiation is directed upwards by the reflex mirror, and the shutter is only exposed to infrared in the instant before it opens to take the picture.

If you want to use High Speed Infrared simply for its ability to penetrate mist very effectively, you must always use a

Processing and printing
Process High Speed Infrared film as quickly as possible after exposure, and if you are doing it yourself, treat the film gently, as the emulsion is comparitively delicate. Stainless steel tanks reduce the risk of fogging to a minimum, though if you do your processing in subdued light, even a plastic tank should prove adequate —run a quick test before you risk an important film, though.

Kodak recommend the use of D-76, D-19 or Microdol-X developers, with processing times of 10 minutes for undiluted D-76, 8 minutes for D-19, and 13 minutes for Microdol-X, all at 20°C with five seconds agitation every minute. If you do not normally use a Kodak developer, your normal black and white developer should be adequate but give 50 to a 100 per cent extra time.

When printing infrared negatives, you may find that a long exposure is necessary, because they are usually denser than panchromatic negatives. The graininess is worse, too, particularly if the film has been overexposed, and the maximum size of print possible from a 35 mm negative is about 20 x 30 cm. Prints larger than this will have very prominent grain.

When printing a particularly dense negative, take care that the edges of the negative do not allow light to flood on to the image area and fog the print. If your enlarger does not have sliding masks below the negative, mask off the clear rebate with red lith tape.

filter to give correct tones, just as with Ektachrome Infrared. The most commonly used filters are Wratten 25 (red), 15 (orange), and 29 or 70 (both deep red). All these allow some visible light to pass, and tones in the final picture are little different from those in the subject.

Because of its extended infrared sensitivity, however, black and white infrared can be used with a visually opaque filter—such as Wratten filters 87, 87C or 88A. These give very strange results—foliage comes out white, and a blue sky is recorded as solid black.

Just as for colour infrared, it can be hard to achieve correct exposure. If you are using a 25 red filter, set your meter to 50 ASA to provide a starting point for calculations for a daylight shot. In

tungsten light, set the dial for 125 ASA. A Wratten 87 filter requires more light, and outdoors an exposure of ASA 25 is more appropriate—set ASA 64 in tungsten light. If you have an SLR with a TTL meter, take readings with the filter removed, as with Ektachrome infrared, or else use a separate, hand-held meter.

Focusing
As infrared wavelengths are longer than visible ones, they are refracted differently by the glass of your lens. As a result, an infrared image normally comes to a focus at a point slightly behind the film plane, when the camera is focused for visible light. This complicates focusing, and if you are forming an image using purely infrared radiation, you must make an adjustment to take this into account.

Most lenses have a red dot on the fixed part of the focusing scale to act as a new focusing index for infrared light. Use this by focusing the image normally, then noting the subject distance on the moving part of the scale. Then shift the focusing ring until this subject distance is aligned with the infrared focusing mark on the lens barrel.

If your lens does not have a special infrared index, it is still easy to focus for infrared light. Focus the camera normally, and then turn the focusing ring as if to focus on a closer object. Keep turning until the subject distance is aligned with the depth of field mark for f/5.6. If you use infrared film frequently, you may wish to put a small mark on the scale at this point—a scratch or a spot of paint.

These special focusing techniques apply only to photography using infrared radiation alone—that is, if you are using a visually opaque filter. Other filters allow at least some visible light to pass through to the film, so the image is formed by a broad range of wavelengths. No ordinary lens can bring all these wavelengths to the same focus, so no one focus setting is appropriate for both visible light and infrared. The only way to cope with this problem is to set the focusing ring to a position halfway between the infrared index and the ordinary focusing index, and then stop down the lens to f/8 or smaller.

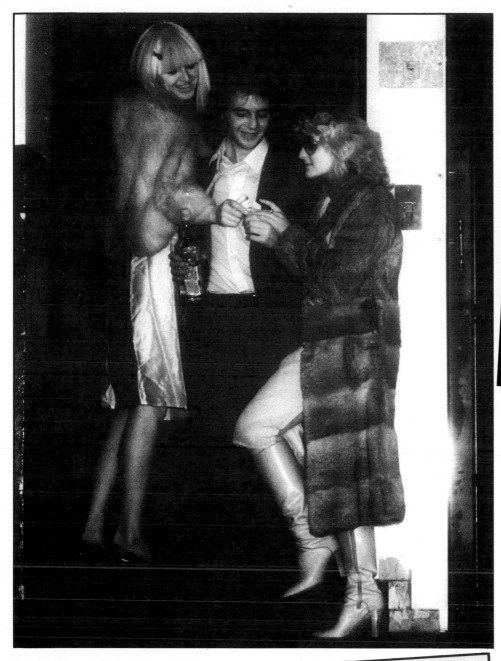

Dark deeds *You can take shots undetected in complete darkness with IR film and an 87 filter over the flash. This cuts out visible light but lets IR through. If the unwitting subjects look directly at the flash they see only a very dim red glow*

Invisible pictures

Because infrared radiation is normally invisible, it is possible to use it to illuminate a scene and take a photograph on infrared film, without anybody in front of the camera being aware of the light. This technique is often used by

> **WARNING**
> Do not be tempted to look at the sun through a visually opaque filter. Although you will not see anything through the filter, harmful infrared radiation passes straight through, and this can quickly damage your eyesight.

police authorities and surveillance agencies, who use it to photograph suspects at night without their knowledge.

Because this technique uses only the infrared sensitivity of the film, it works only with black and white infrared film. On Ektachrome Infrared, it exposes only the cyan-forming layer of the film, and therefore produces just a red image.

Suitable sources of infrared radiation are flashbulbs, floodlights or electronic flash, all of which must be filtered to make sure that they do not emit any visible light. The most practical source of infrared light is a portable electronic flash unit with a Wratten 87 filter over the reflector. The filter makes the flash invisible, except to someone who is looking directly at the reflector, and even they see only a dull red glow.

The filter on the flash cuts the output of your flashgun to about a third of its normal value, and unless you have quite a powerful unit, it may be all but useless with infrared film. As a starting point for exposure settings, you should use the normal guide number for your film, then open up the lens aperture by 1½ stops. You should regard this only as a general guide, and you will have to experiment to determine an accurate guide number for your particular flashgun.

Changing filters *IR Ektachrome does not respond to filtration in the normal way—a yellow filter over the lens, for example, removes a yellow cast when you would expect it to create one*

Copy colour

Creative photographers are always searching for new ways of manipulating their pictures to produce unusual and striking images and, perhaps surprisingly, one of the most interesting tools for this purpose is the colour photocopier. It is, of course, designed simply to produce full colour copies from a variety of originals at the touch of a button, but it can generate brilliantly coloured images from black and white originals: it can make colour copies on clear acetate film: it can produce instant prints from slides, and it can copy three-dimensional objects—even your own face.

Copy bureaux with colour photocopying facilities can be found in most major cities, but access to the machines is variable. Many of the bureaux are run by the two principal manufacturers of copying equipment, Canon and Xerox, and in these places, members of the public are not normally allowed to operate the equipment. Although you can ask the staff to produce copies in a certain way, it is clearly better to experiment yourself if you want unusual creative effects. In this case, you should try to find one of the independent copyshops using Xerox copiers where you may be allowed to operate the machines yourself. The disadvantage is that Xerox machines will only accommodate A4 size originals (210 x 297 mm) and are slightly less faithful in colour reproduction than Canon machines.

To make a straight copy on a Xerox machine, from a colour picture, place the original face down on the glass platen and press the button. The machine then makes the copy by a procedure similar to that which takes place in a conventional black and white machine. Beneath the glass platen, a tubular lamp makes three passes (instead of the usual one per copy). In the course of each pass, an image of a third of a spectrum is formed so that red, green and blue parts of the original are copied in turn. The paper copy is produced by brightly coloured toners—yellow, cyan and magenta powders—which are fused on to the paper by a heating unit. The whole process takes about 15 seconds after which time the copy appears in a slot on top of the machine. It is not necessary to know much more than this about the internal workings of the machine, since everything proceeds automatically, and most adjustments have to be made by a qualified service engineer.

However, all colour copiers incorporate external controls which can be used to manipulate the hue of the final image. Using these, and other less conventional methods, colour casts can be corrected or deliberately introduced to the picture.

The colour balance of the copy is determined by the amounts of magenta, yellow and cyan toner deposited on the paper. The toner densities can be adjusted by three knobs on the control panel of the machine.

Swashbuckling colour *It is easy to produce large areas of pure colour on a copier, either by using coloured originals, or by using the controls to generate colour from black and white*

Daredevil biker *Although a colour copier can make rapid prints from slides, it is unlikely to ever replace the darkroom. In the Xerox print on the far right, colours are more dull and muted than in the original next to it*

The basic rule to remember when making colour corrections is that you reduce a cast in one of the three toner colours—that is, a bias towards either magenta, yellow or cyan—by increasing the density of the other two colours (or reducing the density of the colour causing the cast). If the cast is in one of these three colours, correction is easy enough. Unfortunately most colour casts tend to be a mixture of two of the three colours. The first task, therefore, is to work out which two colours are too strong.

When trying to identify the colours in the cast, remember that a mixture of yellow and magenta makes red, yellow and cyan makes green and cyan and magenta makes blue. So you correct a red cast by increasing the strength of the cyan toner (or reducing the yellow and magenta), a green cast with extra magenta (or reduced yellow and cyan) and a blue cast with extra yellow (or reduced cyan and magenta). Bear in mind that the mixture of the two colours may not be equal, and you may have to alter the strength of one of the two colours creating the cast as well.

The three toner control knobs can be used to adjust density as well as colour. If it is too pale, all the toners should be increased; too dark, and they should all be reduced. It is well worth experimenting quite early on until you obtain a perfect copy, as this experience can prove valuable later—make a note on the back of each copy of the settings of the controls. You may find that copying a Kodak grey scale and colour patches helps you to set the machine up for the kind of copies you prefer. Keep the grey scale and colour patches beside copier for reference when making the copy.

Unusual originals may prove difficult to copy accurately. If they are very light, even setting the toner controls to full power may not provide sufficient density. If this is the case, a neutral density filter placed between the original

Pink room *Colour photocopiers are surprisingly versatile—they lend themselves to photomontage techniques because parts of the picture are easy to reposition, and results can be seen in seconds*

and the glass platen usually provides a satisfactory solution. Large sheets of acrylic neutral density material are available from theatrical lighting suppliers.

Dense originals present the opposite problem. If a satisfactory copy cannot be obtained by reducing the toner supply, the only way to make the copy lighter is to backlight the original. This can really only be done at a self-service copy bureau, and then only with the co-operation of the staff. A convenient light source is the slide projector that is often mounted on Xerox copiers for copying slides, but a more powerful lamp, such as a movie light, works better. The light should be directed so that it gives even coverage over the whole of the copy platen, and should be diffused with tracing paper or translucent plastic.

Contrast control
Contrast is always increased in copying unless special precautions are taken. The increase in contrast can sometimes add graphic impact to a picture, but more often it is a nuisance.

Some copy machines have a contrast regulation dial on the control panel, and this has the effect of adding white to the picture, making the dark areas of the picture lighter. If its limited effect is insufficient, contrast can be further reduced by exposing through a printer's half-tone screen. This helps to retain highlight detail, but results in a copy that has a heavily screened appearance.

Contrast can also be successfully controlled by highlight masking. This technique is complex, but very effective. First, a contact print of the colour original is made in the darkroom at home, and exposure adjusted to give a pale grey image. This negative print is then photocopied on to clear acetate, using a conventional black and white copier. The acetate copy is sandwiched with the colour original to darken its highlights, before copying in colour.

In extreme cases, contrast can be reduced by actually whitening the original with chalk or a fine spray of white paint, though this is obviously nonreversible, and out of the question for a valuable original.

Prints from slides

Besides copying prints and flat artwork, Xerox copiers can also make prints from slides. A special bracket on the side of the machine holds a Kodak Carousel projector which throws an image of the slide being copied through a standard filter pack, and on to a mirror which reflects it down to the glass platen. A half-tone screen is used in contact with the platen to give the picture a full range of tones, and to help illuminate the slide image more evenly.

Before making a print, a white focusing sheet is placed over the half tone screen, and the size and focus of the projected image is adjusted using the projector's zoom lens. The focus paper is removed, and an initial test copy is made with all the copier controls set to 'normal' values. On the basis of the test, exposures can be adjusted using a 'lighten/darken' control on the projector, and colour

balance can be changed with the toner knobs, or by placing extra filters in front of the projector lens.

Creative techniques

Once you have mastered simple colour copying, you can begin to exploit the ability of colour copiers to manipulate images and to create colour from black and white originals. You can manipulate the copy image to produce numerous different effects and the best way to produce original images is to experiment for yourself, but there are a number of basic manipulations to begin with.

Colour from black and white By using the single colour mode of the copier, you can generate coloured images from black and white originals. The Canon copier has a range of only six colours, but on the Xerox machines, the pallet is much wider—you can 'dial in' the colour you want just by turning the toner dials. Apart from the change of mode in the copier (which is accomplished at the flip of a switch) colour from black and white copies are made in the normal way.

Copies on acetate This facility is available on both types of machine, though not as a self-serve facility. This means that the cost is higher than for self-serve paper copies. The transparencies that are produced are intended for overhead projection, but they have other possibilities for a photographer. They can be used as transparent overlays, and combined with other images to produce colour photomontage without the necessity of cutting up any of the picture elements.

Posterization You can also use the copier to make brilliant poster-like pictures in three colours from black and white originals with the aid of tone separations. Tone separations are simply three ver-

Butterfly fantasy *Iridescent colours can be generated by moving the original between passes of the copier light bar*

sions of the original printed onto lith film in the darkroom—only one is overexposed, one correctly exposed and the other under exposed. If you have darkroom skills, you can make the separations yourself; otherwise you may find a professional lab to make them for you. To make the posterized picture, you simply copy each of the three separations in a different colour, varying the density of each colour, or the colour you print each separation, to achieve the effect you want.

Copying solid objects The copier lens has a depth of field extending about five centimetres above the platen. Thus small objects such as fruit, clothing, flowers and jewellery can all be 'copied' successfully. They can be arranged to form collages, or combined with prints to form a montage. By removing the objects between passes of the light bar, they can be made to appear in only one or two of the three primary colours.

If you can keep sufficiently still between each of the three exposures, you can even make colour copies of your face in the same way. Any movement of hair or eyelashes shows up as rainbow colours on the final copy.

Copier limitations

Probably the biggest limitation on the use of colour copiers is the accuracy with which they reproduce the spectrum. They work best with bright primary colours, and less well with pastel shades, flesh tones and earth colours. Even these, however, copy well just after the machine has been serviced. With a little practice, you can soon learn what sort of images are likely to reproduce well all the time.

Posterization with a copier

Colour copiers build up an image by recording the three primary colours one by one. If you put a different black and white image on the platen for the duration of each pass of the light bar, you can build up a full colour image. In this case, line separations were made in the darkroom by the process described in the text. The first was copied as pure cyan, and then quickly switched for the second, which was copied as yellow. This in turn was replaced by the third, which formed a magenta image.

You must be nimble fingered to switch the sheets over—there is only a two second break between colours—and the dimensions of each line separation must be identical, or the coloured images will not be in exact register

Chapter 4
FILTER EFFECTS
Creative filtering

Many photographers believe that instant creative photography lies no further from their grasp than the special effects filters in the bottom of their gadget bags. If it were as simple as that then everyone's collection would be brimming with creative masterpieces—but the reality is very different; truly creative shots, with or without filters, are hard to take.

However, filters do have a place in creative photography but it is important to realize that special effects alone will not do the job for you. When you are about to reach for a filter, you should already have answered an important question—'why does this photograph need it?' Basically, there are two answers. To produce an unusual or attractively different image from the already good picture you see before you; or to make something of a subject that, without a filter, does not stand up as a good shot in its own right. Whatever the case, you should always assess first the merits of a scene without a filter.

More than anything, creative filtering needs a subtle touch: the filter should never draw attention to itself. If the first reaction to your pictures is 'Ah! that was taken with such and such a filter', you can be sure you have overdone the filtering.

Clearly, then, the more dramatic special effects filters should be used sparingly. Indeed, it is often the mundane filters that are most valuable

creatively, allowing you to make small but nonetheless effective adjustments to the image in the viewfinder. Many photographers use colour balancing and compensation filters, for instance, only in situations where the ambient light and the film are in some way incompatible. But these filters can be used to subtly alter the colouring even in a scene where no correction is necessary.

In scenes where the colours are generally pale, for instance, you can often give pictures extra impact by strengthening the colours already present with a coloured filter. Warming filters in the 81 series are particularly useful in this respect, because people are naturally attracted to warm colours. Portraits by electronic flash in particular can benefit from subtle warming. Although flash gives technically correct colour with daylight film, it tends to look a little cold and a warming filter over the lens or flashgun helps considerably. But warming filters can also be used to 'improve' natural light.

When the sun is weak in winter, or when the vegetation is bleached by the heat of midsummer, landscapes can seem pale and insipid. A mild warming filter helps to bring out the colour. Even when the natural lighting or colouring is already warm—during the late afternoon or in autumn, for instance—you could use a warming filter to exaggerate the

warmth and bathe the landscape in a rich, golden glow.

But it is important not to overdo it—a filter that warms up the landscape nicely may take all the sparkle and freshness from a blue sky. Try to make sure that the filtration is in sympathy with the scene and, to start with at least, use filters only where the result is 'realistic' or plausible. A yellowish sky looks attractive when the sun is low at dusk, but distinctly odd when it is overhead at midday.

Nevertheless, with a little thought, you can sometimes use strong warming filters 'unrealistically' to create a particular mood or feeling. For shots into the sun or for scenes with strong contrasts, a strong warming filter tends to create the impression of heat—a barren white rockscape might take on the heat of a desert: an unexotic North Sea beach may have the feel of a tropical shore. In other situations light brown or even sepia filters can help to evoke the warm golden glow of summers past—ideal for a nostalgic shot of a veteran car or an old country cottage. But remember to exclude things that might look strange in sepia. Again, it is also important to be sparing in your use of filters—people will soon get bored if all your pictures are brown.

Cooling filters are slightly harder to use, perhaps because blues are generally less attractive in pictures than warmer colours. Nevertheless, they too can be useful creative tools. A standard technique in misty weather, for instance, is to use a warming filter to take away some of the blueness such as an 81C. But sometimes, particularly in heavy mist over water, you can create a more unusual picture by using a cooling filter to emphasize the blueness. Although clearly not realistic, the result may have a deep, shining, dreamlike quality. Similarly in snow scenes, where there are no recognizable colours to upset the effect, you can use a blue filter to accentuate the blue and create an impression of coldness. But again it is important to remember that because you are colouring the whole image, the effect can look odd if the picture is anything but very simple—any colours, such as yellow, will generally look unpleasant with a blue cast.

Taking cooling a little further, you can use a deep blue filter, combined with a polarizer and a stop or two under-exposure, to mimic the 'day for night' effect popular in early movie making—when filters were used to give an impression of night in a daytime shoot. Any highlights in the picture are muted and take on a blue cast—the sky should

Purple haze *Simple subjects are most amenable to filtering. Here, a graduated filter turns a lone figure in a snowscape into a moody and effective study*

Office block *Since this abstract scene was monochrome, two graduated filters were fitted. Both were angled to match the overall composition*

Obelisk *Special effects filters have been overworked and results can be dull, but here the star-crossed streetlamp nicely complements the floodlit obelisk*

be a deep navy blue—while the contrast range is also reduced to give an impression of a moonlit night. This can be particularly effective in wooded areas or on a tropical beach with palm trees framing the foreground. If the sun is included in the frame, it can sometimes look like a bright full moon.

Cooling and warming filters are not the only filters available for adjusting the colour balance in a picture. There are many other colours—indeed, any colour you care to choose. Each of these can be, with imagination and a light touch, used to manipulate the colour of a scene to achieve a certain effect. But the number

of occasions on which these more usual colours are appropriate is far more limited, because casts in these colous are much more disturbing than either warm or cold casts—they are not associated with any natural lighting.

Filters must be chosen very carefully to match each subject, and there are no general rules. But a few examples may give an idea of the possibilities. You can subtly reduce the colourless look of snow scenes, for instance, with a very pale magenta filter. A pale magenta filter can also put a bit of colour in insipid looking brickwork. A strong magenta filter, on the other hand, can be used to

Bridge *If there is a definite horizontal break in the middle of the frame, you can use a two-coloured filter—here red and blue—but the effect is rarely subtle*

Racing the moon *With a deep blue filter and underexposure, you can create a 'moonlit night'. To complete the effect, you can sandwich it with a slide of the moon*

With the right holder, graduated filters can be manoeuvred so that only a small part of the frame or virtually all of it is filtered. The graduated transition zone prevents any hard, obvious lines.

Landscapes, cityscapes, seascapes and many other outdoor pictures frequently include a large area of sky. If the sky is weak and pale, it tends to weaken the whole picture. Sometimes you can frame to exclude most of the sky from the frame. But where you cannot, or do not wish to do this, you can use a graduated filter—either a neutral density to darken the sky and emphasize the clouds, or a filter to put colour in the sky—with the transition zone aligned with the horizon.

Normally you would choose the colour to suit the sky and retain the existing mood, but one of the attractions of graduated filters is that you can put a wide variety of colours in the sky to create a different mood or effect. A heavy brown or tobacco filter, for instance, could be used to create a dramatic stormy look on a dull, cloudy day. Shooting into the sun through an

give an aura of glamour to cities at dusk. The filter puts a little colour in the sky and grey buildings and helps to reduce the colour differences between various light sources.

Because of the psychological associations of the colour, shots through a red filter tend to have an air of tension or oppressive heat. Consequently, many photographers who wish to create this kind of mood—especially in city shots—have resorted to strong red filters, giving pictures in which highlights are red and shadows are black. Shots like this are now something of a cliché and their impact is reduced. Nevertheless, the approach does work occasionally. If you do try this kind of shot, remember that detail tends to be lost and only strong dark shapes show up. So keep to very simple, perhaps silhouetted, shapes or shoot on a misty day when a few dramatic shapes loom out of the mist.

Except perhaps for silhouettes, strong filters should be avoided with portraits and shots including people. Most people have a very strong image of skin colour and any unnatural colouring tends to look very unpleasant. Perhaps the exception to this rule is female nudes because photographs long ago abandoned 'standard' treatments in order to find a new way of looking at a 'traditional' subject. Consequently, we have been exposed so much to female nudes in outlandish situations and colours that even the weirdest colouring no longer seems strange. But precisely because of this constant exposure, strongly filtered nude shots need particularly good composition if they are not to look dull.

Although there clearly are times when strongly coloured filters can be used to create an attractive shot, their value is generally limited because they colour the whole picture. While an all-red or all-green picture might seem unusual and exciting at first, the effect soon palls. Perhaps the most useful creatively of all filters, therefore, are graduated filters.

Promenade *On a dull day when the sky is weak and pale, a strong graduated filter—here tobacco—can make all the difference, creating a dramatic, stormy mood in a normal seaside scene*

Skier *Multiple image filters are very popular but only with the right subject do they have anything but novelty value. Here, with a simple, dynamic subject the multiple image creates a feeling of action and movement*

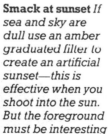

Smack at sunset *If sea and sky are dull use an amber graduated filter to create an artificial sunset—this is effective when you shoot into the sun. But the foreground must be interesting*

amber graduated filter, you can create a sunset effect.

Photographers tend to use graduated filters only to compensate for a weak sky, but there is no reason why they cannot be used for other purposes. In a cityscape, for instance, the background buildings might look pale and unexciting—a graduated filter in a colour in sympathy with the stonework might help to complete the picture or create a particular mood. If the foreground is pale and weak, on the other hand, you could turn a graduated filter upside down. A snow scene might benefit from an inverted pale magenta graduated filter; a tobacco filter might improve a shot across parched ploughed fields or a cornfield. Indeed, there is no reason why you cannot hold the graduated filter in any place or at any angle to put colour in a weak area of the picture—although usually only horizontal alignments look natural. But it is important to choose the colour of the filter to suit the subject and avoid using unnecessary extremes.

With a little care, you can combine two graduated filters in the same picture to achieve even more interesting effects. You could, for instance, use a grey and a blue filter overlapping over the sky so that the sky gradually darkens upward from the horizon: a pink and a blue could create a sunset effect. Alternatively, you can combine the filters in opposition so that one affects the sky and the other affects the foreground. This is particularly useful where the main point of interest is just a narrow band across the centre of the frame—such as a line of trees or a pier at the seaside.

Sometimes you may want a very marked transitional zone between the two filters: at others you may need a less distinct transition. You can control the nature of the transition through your placing of the filters and your choice of lens and aperture. With a wide angle lens and a narrow aperture, the transition tends to be fairly abrupt; with a telephoto and a wide aperture, the transition tends to be smoother.

Effects filters

Most amateurs are familiar with the use of filters to modify a light source or to achieve faithful rendition of colours. Also intended for the amateur market are filters for special effects, ranging in complexity from simple coloration, through selective magnification to distortion of the image. Before you attempt to use these, it is best to know what effect they give and how easily it is achieved.

Special effects filters are available separately or in kits, and vary in price according to the construction. In the Cokin range, for example, a coloured diffuser costs less than a plastic lens cap, and a 'diffraction universe' costs about the same as a 36 exposure roll of Koda-chrome. For about four times as much you can buy a Hoyarex starter kit, complete with Hoya filters and acces-

sories for attaching them to the camera lens.

The basis of the various special effects filter systems is a filter holder, which is attached to the camera lens by an adapter ring that screws into the filter thread. A range of adapters is supplied with some filter systems, but with others you must ensure you buy the correct adapter for your lens.

Filters are slotted into the holder in grooves, which vary in distance from the front of the lens. Filters from one system will not fit into a holder from another system, so it is a good idea to decide on one make only.

Some filters are no more than a shape cut out of black cardboard to form a mask. You can make these simply, to your own design, but the effect is

Filter kits *include a range of basic filters and accessories—some of which are not strictly necessary*

probably not worth the effort. Most special effect filters are outside the scope of the do-it-yourself enthusiast, but you can appreciate the effects better by studying how the filters work.

Probably the most sophisticated filters work by diffraction. These are gratings made from high quality optical glass ruled with parallel lines in one or more directions—they give a star or coloured spot effect. Easily the most creative filters are the Coloured Vaseline and Coloured Varnishes, with which a wide range of coloured effects can be achieved. But they can be a little difficult to handle.

The rainbow effect *is most prominent when this type of subject (a bright sky and reflective water surface) is underexposed. At the correct exposure, the rainbow is 'washed out'. In a real rainbow, the colours occur in the reverse order*

Spot in violet *Essentially this is a diffuser with a clear central spot. There is a choice of several different colours, and the filter can be combined with others, such as a starburst. Focusing through the filter can be a problem*

A split field filter *is merely half a lens in a mount, used as a close-up lens for half the field of view. The edge of the lens causes blurring, and the non-uniform magnification causes distortion, as can be seen in the upper shot*

Coloured diffuser *This is supplied as two squares of crumpled plastic, which vary in colour according to the angle of view you use. Shown above are shots with and without the filter*

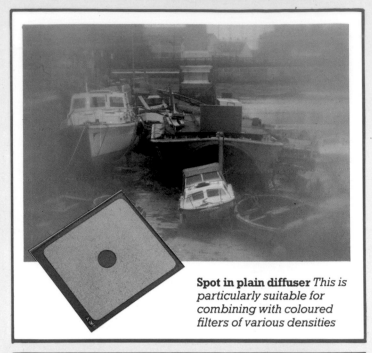

Spot in plain diffuser *This is particularly suitable for combining with coloured filters of various densities*

Dreams *The effect varies enormously according to the aperture used and the filter to lens distance*

Diffraction universe *These are plain in appearance, but are in fact extremely fine gratings of various designs*

Coloured varnish, *smeared on to glass, gives a varied effect. Here it is used to tint the night sky*

Starburst *filters for point light sources—available for two, four, eight or 16 rays*

Masks *come in a variety of shapes, but you can easily make them yourself*

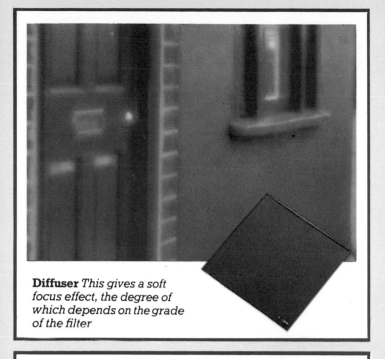

Diffuser *This gives a soft focus effect, the degree of which depends on the grade of the filter*

A graduated diffuser *leaves part of the image sharp, so it is easily combined with other coloured filters*

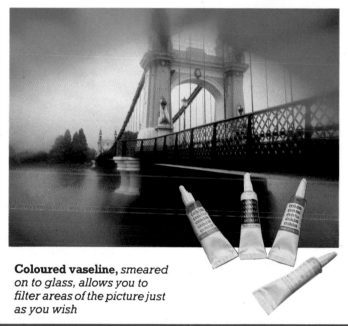

Coloured vaseline, *smeared on to glass, allows you to filter areas of the picture just as you wish*

Fog filters *are similar to diffusers. Their effect varies according to the density of the coating on each filter*

Linear slit *This is probably the most difficult filter to use (see page 90) but the easiest to make yourself. Results depend on how smoothly you wind the film*

Soft focus

Sharp, crisp pictures are the sort of photographs most people want to produce. Manufacturers go to a lot of trouble to produce lenses that give the finest possible detail. The viewfinders on many modern cameras incorporate split prisms and other devices to aid precision focusing.

Yet sometimes the picture demands another approach, a different way of presenting the subject. This is where soft focus comes in. By gently diffusing some, or all, of the image a different mood or response is evoked in the mind of the viewer.

Unfortunately, as with all special techniques, there is a tendency for some photographers to overdo it or to use soft focus where it is completely inappropriate. This has given the technique a bad name with some people. They see it merely as a cosmetic treatment for otherwise weak pictures. Such an attitude ignores the fact that many fine pictures have been created in this way. The important thing is to use soft focus in a controlled way where it will create the effect you want.

When to use it

Soft focus originally came into use around the turn of the century when it was used to create photographs that imitated the paintings fashionable at the time. However, it did not take long

Overall diffusion *Strong soft focus obscures skin detail and creates an overall glowing effect*

Pseudo soft focus *A shallow depth of field has been used to mimic true soft focus in this flower shot*

Concentrating attention *Leaving the centre clear focuses attention on important details*

before it was realized that if it was used when photographing the fashionable women of the day, it would create a very glamorous effect. This is still one of its main uses today.

In fact, professional photographers tend to use soft focus whenever they want to make a subject particularly attractive and it is frequently used in fashion, glamour, advertising and food photography.

Most amateurs seem to use this approach for portraits, though there is plenty of scope for soft focus in other areas. The original use in landscapes is one of these. By obscuring fine details, the scene becomes more generalized so that it is composed of broad shapes. This can help if you wish to emphasize the beauty of the scene rather than record information about a place.

It can also be used when shooting the bright lights of a city at night. In this situation it further emphasizes the glow of the strong colours in the darkness.

Soft focus while shooting
There are a number of different ways of achieving soft focus in the camera. A translucent material, such as fine gauze, nylon stocking or glass smeared with a petroleum jelly such as Vaseline, can be placed between the lens and the subject. Alternatively a special filter or lens attachment, or even a special soft focus lens, is used on the camera when the picture is being shot. These devices scatter the light in the same way as mist or fog scatters the light from a street lamp. Not only do the fine details merge but the light diffuses outwards from the highlight areas creating a faint glow round them.

Such diffusion also reduces the contrast range of the image compared to the original scene. It is therefore sensible to select subjects that feature strongly contrasting areas. Diffusing subjects that lack contrast will create images that merely look flat.

Clear detail *A good example of how too much detail can destroy the mood of a shot. The background also distracts the eye from the centre of interest, which is the shell rather than the sea*

Atmosphere *By using soft focus irrelevant detail is obscured and a sense of mystery is created. It also emphasizes the basic shapes*

Simple soft focus
To begin with, the easiest way to create a soft focus effect, without going to any great expense, is to smear Vaseline on to a piece of thin glass or on to a spare UV filter.

There are two rules to observe when using Vaseline. Most importantly, never smear it directly on to the lens. Even if you manage to remove it the lens coating may well be irreparably damaged. Secondly, always use a very fine film of Vaseline. If you are using a 35 mm camera, either a print or a projected slide involves a considerable degree of magnification. Thus any effect created in the camera can end up looking rather crude unless care is exercised during shooting.

When spreading the Vaseline, remember that the direction in which you move your finger, whether in a circular fashion or in a series of straight lines radiating out from the centre, will affect the final result. Even the finest marks will create patterns in the diffused areas. Thus random movements of the hand should be avoided for this will create a chaotic set of diffusion lines.

How much diffusion
At some point you will need to decide whether you wish to diffuse the entire image, smearing all the glass, or only part of it, leaving a hole in the middle. Overall diffusion will appear soft and dreamlike but a clear centre will allow a contrast between sharp and diffused details to be created. By aligning the clear area with an important part of the image you can direct attention to it in a quite striking way.

The size of the clear patch is best determined in relation to the subject by trial and error. With SLR cameras the most effective balance between diffused and clear areas can be determined visually. If you do not have this facility you will have to make some trial exposures and judge the effect in the finished results. When doing this, begin by covering the edge of the image and gradually work inwards with each test until only a small spot is left.

The diffuser-to-lens distance
If you smear Vaseline on to an old or spare UV filter you will be able to screw it into the front of the lens easily. This overcomes the inconvenience of holding the diffuser during exposure. Such attachments cannot be moved away from the lens to vary the diffusion effect because the rim of the filter, being the same diameter as the lens, will soon obscure the corners of the image and cause vignetting.

If you coat the Vaseline on to a larger piece of glass it can be moved from the lens to vary the effect. However, care must be taken to avoid picking up reflections on the rear surface of the glass that will interfere with the image. A tube made of rolled black paper between the diffuser and the camera lens will prevent such reflections.

Special effects

Occasionally you will find a subject with which you can use the smearing of the Vaseline in a quite deliberate way to create a particular effect. By using a thicker layer of Vaseline and applying it in one direction the effect of rain or even shafts of sunlight can be created.

Other diffusing materials

As already indicated, fabrics, such as fine gauze or nylon stocking, can be used to diffuse the image. Always use white or pale tints as these will scatter the light. Dark materials will merely absorb it.

Materials, particularly nylon, can easily be stretched over the front of the lens and held in place by their own elasticity. However, this can easily obscure the focusing and aperture rings. It is more convenient to fix them to a filter holder, such as that used by the Cokin and similar systems.

When using nylon the degree of diffusion can be changed by stretching the material to a greater or lesser extent. It is also a simple matter to create clear areas by making holes in the nylon material.

Aperture and exposure

Changing the size of the aperture has an effect on the amount of diffusion that occurs. Not only does the diffusing material scatter the light rays that create the image, but it also picks up stray cross light from beyond the edge of the image area and deflects it into the

camera. Obviously such deflections are going to occur more frequently round the edge of the lens. Thus, when the aperture is stopped down and the light is only passing through the centre of the lens, there is less opportunity for these deflections to occur.

In addition, only those rays passing through the centre of the lens will form the image when a small aperture is used. Those that have been more widely scattered will be stopped by the leaves of the aperture diaphragm. So if you wish to have the maximum amount of diffusion, you should work with the aperture open to its full extent.

Generally speaking, if you use the improvized soft focus techniques as

Colour shapes By diffusing the details of the foliage, attention is concentrated on the shape of the colour areas

described, you should not need to alter your exposure. However, those with cameras incorporating through the lens metering systems or automatic exposure control may experience minor exposure problems. As already indicated, the diffusing material deflects light into the lens from outside the image area, thus misleading the meter into giving a false reading. So, if you do experience slight underexposure when using soft focus, increase the amount of light reaching the film by up to one stop.

Soft focus filters and attachments

Inexpensive soft focus filters, that can be screwed on the front of the lens or attached by means of a separate holder, are now available in a variety of types that give a number of slightly different effects. Their main advantage is that the effect is consistent from one occasion to another. They are also quicker and more convenient to use than the improvized methods. The disadvantage is that you cannot create the subtle variations possible with fabric or Vaseline. However,

Shape A Cokin fog filter obscures fine detail and also emphasizes the shape of the tree

Backgrounds Here a black stocking diffuses highlight areas beyond the lorry to cut out distracting detail

Windmill *By making clear emphatic marks in the Vaseline an otherwise dull area is given interest*

Cottage *A thinly smeared centre and a thick outer area create flare that enhances the 'olde worlde' effect*

Blurred building *Really strong streaking reduces the subject to a series of indistinct shapes*

some systems allow you to combine filters and so vary the degree of softness in the image.

These filters are either Perspex or glass with a very lightly grained surface that creates the diffusion. Some have clear centre spots that allow the contrast effects between sharp and soft areas already discussed. Their effect on exposure is the same as that for improvised filters. Again the size of the aperture affects the degree of diffusion.

Much more expensive soft focus attachments are available that fit on to the front of the lens. The best known is the Zeiss Softar series designed for Hasselblad cameras. A set of three is available that give an increasing amount of diffusion as you pass from numbers 1 to 3. However, no variation is possible as

with the cheaper systems and the cost is such that their purchase can only really be justified by the professional user.

Soft focus lenses

In the past, when these effects were much in demand by professional portrait photographers, a number of manufacturers made this type of lens. They still turn up fairly frequently on the secondhand market. However, most were designed for use with studio cameras. Of the large manufacturers, both Fuji and Minolta still make these lenses for 35 mm cameras.

Most soft focus lenses work by combining uncorrected lens distortions with a specially designed aperture plate that exaggerates the softening effect. The more you stop down, the smaller the

amount of diffusion created.

The Minolta Vari-Soft works in a different way. The relative positions of the glass elements inside the lens are changed by means of a ring. The disadvantage of all these lenses is their expense, which may be considered to be out of proportion to any advantages that they might have over the cheaper filters.

No matter which method you decide to use, the soft focus technique can produce very pleasing effects. But do not be tempted to use it too often otherwise it will lose its impact and you will find that your photographs lack variety. Remember that a soft focus treatment must suit the subject—the colours and light must be soft too—or the picture can easily look as if it is merely badly focused. Use it to enhance atmosphere, not disguise faults.

Chapter 5
MIXING IMAGES
Front and back projection

You do not need to go to the Caribbean to shoot a friend on a tropical beach or to France to picture a bottle of Bordeaux in an 'authentic' setting. You can put all kinds of backgrounds, exotic and mundane, in your pictures without moving from your studio simply by projecting a slide of the scene on to a screen behind the subject.

Slides can be projected either from behind the screen (back projection) or from in front, with the projector close to the camera (front projection). Although you can buy sophisticated—and expensive—equipment designed especially for background projection, you can achieve quite acceptable results using just a normal slide projector.

Most projection techniques are straightforward and the problems occur more in the choice of suitable slides, equipment and the lighting arrangement rather than in taking the shot. Although

there are a number of different approaches, certain principles of projection apply to all the methods.

Projection principles

When using either back projection or front projection, it is important to prevent light from the studio lamps falling on to the screen or projection surface. Light spillage of this kind reduces the contrast and colour saturation of the background image. Barn doors, snoots and other masks should be used on the lights to direct the light on to the subject while shielding the screen.

Unless you are using an abstract or obviously non-realistic background it is also important to match the direction and quality of the lighting on the subject with that of the background slide. This may mean using colour balancing filters on the projector to match the colour of the studio lighting.

Matching the lighting in the studio with the lighting in the slide can often be very difficult, particularly if the lighting in the slide is strongly directional. If the scene in the slide is lit by strong sunlight, you may find it impossible to match the angle and intensity in the studio without spilling light onto the projection screen. For this reason, it is usually better to choose a slide in which the lighting is fairly diffuse. With soft lighting, the direction of the light source is much less obvious, and it is much easier to disguise any differences.

For the same reason, it is usually easier to work with slides in which the colours are fairly muted. People expect background colours to be less bright anyway, and it is far easier achieving a match with soft colours than with strong.

Moonlit sky *Front and back projection are most useful for producing surreal or slightly abstract pictures*

Perspectives in both the subject and screen image must also match. This is especially important if perspective lines are continued or repeated in the background. A shot looking down on a model posed in front of a picture of a street scene shot from ground level would not look right. The match will also look better if the slide and studio shot are both taken with the same lens.

Scale also plays an important part here, and you must adjust the image until it is precisely the right size for the subject. If your projector has a zoom lens, you can simply zoom in or out to achieve the right scale. Otherwise, you must move either the projector, the screen or the subject.

Background shots taken on wide angle lenses show an exaggerated distortion toward the sides, especially of strong vertical lines like the edges of buildings. This can be used creatively, but for most applications the background should be distortion free. Ideally, the camera lens should have an angle of view as close to that of the background slide as possible. In fact, the foreshortening effect of a longer than normal lens is often preferred, not only for a tighter image but also because the depth of field is shallower and the inevitable separation of foreground and background looks more natural and not so contrived.

If the background is intended to be far distant, too much depth of field in the slide may ruin the effect—it is sometimes a good idea to have the background out of focus. Do not use a slide with the foreground out of focus or the composite will have two points of focus. The slides used should also be in glass mounts to prevent them from buckling. It is also a good idea to use the largest format possible so that the effect is not ruined by grain—6 × 6 cm slides are ideal.

Projection techniques can be used to

Back projection *The shots above show a basic set-up—using a standard projector and a translucent screen—and the type of result you can easily obtain*

Combined images *The small shots below show the components which are combined to form the main picture. Note how grey the screen is without an image on it*

recreate the view through a window or door in an interior shot. In this case, the perfect match between the projected image and the main subject is not so important. The studio lighting on the subject does not have to match with the daylight in the slide, for instance, and you can use a wider angle lens. But, depending on the brightness of the exterior and the direction of the sunlight, it may be necessary to backlight the subject to simulate the light coming through the window.

Front projection
The simplest and cheapest technique is front projection using a standard slide projector to throw an image on to a white surface, such as background paper. The subject is placed in front of this image and lit separately using tungsten or quartz lights, to match the light source of

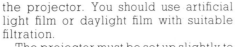

the projector. You should use artificial light film or daylight film with suitable filtration.

The projector must be set up slightly to one side so that it projects *behind* the subject, otherwise the image will show up on the subject as well. This causes some distortion of the image, and so the original picture must be chosen with this in mind. Either use a picture which does not suffer when distorted slightly, such as a landscape, or use the distortion to create interesting effects. Unless you want abstract effects, make the angle between the camera and the projector as small as possible, not only to minimize distortions, but to avoid problems with focusing the projector lens.

If you take background shots specifically for this type of projection, you can try shooting scenes with at least one dark area. With the projector near the camera, you can project the slide directly on to the screen and the subject, with the latter placed so that it is in the dark area of the image. However, although simple, this approach does tend to be rather limiting.

A much more sophisticated and versatile system uses a special projector and screen. This is the type of front projection used by professionals. The projector, which is usually set pointing vertically upwards, throws the image on to a semi-silvered mirror set at 45° in front of the camera lens. This reflects it on to the screen and subject. The camera 'sees' through the mirror, so that the projector beam and camera view are on exactly the same axis and the shadows cast by the subject are directly behind it and out of view.

The screen that should be used is a beaded, high gain type which has a very high reflectance and a narrow reflectance angle. This means that the image on the screen is very bright—much brighter than the image falling on the subject. When the film is exposed for the screen, the image on the subject is very underexposed so that very little of it

Lighting set-up *Note how the lights in the front projection set-up above are positioned and shielded to avoid light reaching the screen. Backlighting is used (bottom) to remove a black line on the shoulder (top) caused by fringing*

can be seen. Furthermore, when the subject is lit separately, all remaining traces of the projected image are washed out.

Professional units such as the Bowens Front/Pro, use a flash head in the projector to make the exposure, though a modelling light is included for viewing. This means that you can use studio flash units to light the subject. These lights must be kept out of the reflective area of the screen which is roughly 20° to 30° each side of the camera/projector axis, depending on the particular screen.

Although these units are very expensive (the screens alone can cost as much as a roll film SLR), it is possible to hire them, and some studios offer them as additional facilities. The better models have the projector, mirror (or beamsplitter) and camera mount contained in the same unit. This is important as the camera lens and projector beam must be accurately aligned. If they are not the **result is a black line, known as** *fringing,* round the subject caused by shadows, and producing a 'cardboard cut-out' effect. Front projection systems which have the various components separate can take some time to set up, and accurate alignment is often difficult.

Once the units are set up, they are very easy to use. But to get the best out of them there are a few techniques you can use. For example, it is a good idea to have your subject between one and two metres from the screen. This gives enough separation to allow you to light the subject without spillage on to the screen, but without causing depth of field problems.

Even with properly aligned units, some fringing may occur. To overcome this you should use some backlighting,

and possibly some toplighting too. This lightens the edges of the subject, and with some surfaces, such as pale materials or skin, slight flaring often occurs, which improves the image.

Beware of using a camera angle and composition which includes the feet of a standing person. As there is no shadow coming from the feet, the effect is to make the person look as though he or she is floating.

Back projection
Similar problems can occur with back projection. This is the technique which was widely employed in movie work, and is still sometimes used. The advantage of back projection is that it produces results almost as good as those of sophisticated front projection systems, but using much cheaper equipment. The disadvantage is that you need considerable space behind the screen to give a large enough image. It is sometimes necessary to reflect the projector beam off a 45° mirror, or zig-zag i

between several mirrors, to cut down on the required space.

With back projection there is no danger of your subject casting shadows or producing fringing. But it is necessary to choose your screen material very carefully if you are not to create other problems.

A wide variety of screens and other materials can be used, to varying degrees of success. Professional back projection screens, as used for movie work and audio–visual displays, are made of acrylic substrates (or glass) which diffuse light evenly (so preventing 'hot spots') and absorb ambient front light. They are supplied in neutral grey and white, as well as a range of tints, and are designed for daylight use. However, the areas behind the screen must be dark if you are to get a bright, detailed and reasonably contrasty image.

As with all non-rigid screens, the material should be stretched tight so that there are no wrinkles, which would otherwise show in the final picture. For this reason, the larger screens are laced

be used effectively as backgrounds for small scale still-lifes.

Alternatively, you can make your own screen. Various types of material are available, including a special back projection type, which comes in rolls 1.6 m wide. If a proper screen is not available, sheets of Kodatrace or matt celluloid can be used, as long as they are wrinkle free.

Unfortunately, many materials which might seem suitable for back projection have either a texture or a grain structure. This can show up clearly if the screen is sharply in focus in the final picture. Although it might not matter with abstract backgrounds it makes a realistic effect impossible.

A more difficult problem to overcome is that of hot spots. Proper back projection materials diffuse the light to give even brightness across the whole screen area. Hot spots are reduced by having a thicker screen, but this also cuts down the light level. It is a good idea to experiment with different materials to find the best one for your purposes.

As with the simpler type of front projection, tungsten or quartz lights should be used to light the subject. A few, special back projection systems are available which feature electronic flash sources in the projector. But these are prohibitively expensive for the amateur. Unless you are using a special daylight screen, be careful to shield the screen from the studio lights to prevent a washed-out look. Transparencies taken for back projection should also be of fairly high contrast to compensate for any wash-out remaining. Any type of projector can be used, but space usually dictates a shortish focal length lens, or a mirror system.

Once the equipment is set up, the photography is quite straightforward. Normal metering methods can be used, but for complete control, especially with systems using flash, it is an advantage to have a camera to which a Polaroid back can be fitted. This allows you to check the effect, especially the relative light levels of subject and screen image, before shooting conventional film.

Projection gear
Front projection units (left) use semi-silvered mirrors to throw the image on to the subject. To ensure correct alignment, the camera lens is clamped in place. You can also get good results with simple equipment (right and below). In this case, the image was thrown on to black paper

on to a frame like a trampoline. If a full-length studio shot is set up, the floor in front of the screen may have to be built up to hide the frame.

Screens of this type can be expensive, but there are cheaper alternatives. 3M make a portable *Polacoat* twin screen unit which carries both front and rear projection screens snapped into a light-weight frame. Table top screens designed for audio–visual displays can

Montage

Of all the techniques available to the photographer, few provide more scope for both serious creative work and sheer fun than photomontage. By simply cutting out selected areas of prints and pasting them down on others, you can create a wide range of pictorial effects.

Obviously, the effectiveness of each montage depends upon your choice of pictures and your skill in cutting them up and pasting them down. Once you have mastered the basics, however, the potential for photomontage is limited only by your imagination and the materials you choose to use.

When you assemble a montage, you can take one of two approaches: you can either try to disguise the joins between the various elements, suggesting that the picture is a single photograph; or you can deliberately show up the joins using a rough cut technique. Rough cut montages are undoubtedly easier to make because they need less skill and care in cutting and pasting, though the results can often be very satisfying. They will look very obviously like montages, but there is nothing wrong with this. Deliberate emphasis of the difference between the various elements of the montage lends a surreal quality often exploited by modern cartoonists sometimes to devastating effect.

Rough cut

When you first start to make a montage, it is a good idea to select a photograph to provide the background first and then try superimposing a variety of subjects on it. As you become more skilled at judging suitable montage material, you may prefer to work the other way round, looking for backgrounds to suit a chosen subject.

Once you have selected the background photograph, make a print large enough to work on easily—at least 50 cm × 40 cm—and mount it on stiff card. The other images are eventually pasted on to this print, so make as neat a job as you can.

After you have made the background print, you make prints of the other images that are to be mounted on to it. These prints must be correctly pro-

Smelter *Although simple principles are involved, this montage is a combination of several images which form a coherent and interesting arrangement*

'A B C D' 1923 *A montage—almost a collage—of cuttings and photographs make up this image. You could do much the same using photos and newspapers*

portioned to the background to create the effect you want. If you wish to mount a series of figures realistically on to a recognizable background, for instance, the prints of the figures must clearly be the appropriate size. To make sure you get the size right, cover the background print with tracing paper and trace the outlines of the main features in felt tip pen. Be careful not to press hard with the pen or you may mark the print. Place the finished tracing on your enlarger baseboard and project your chosen subject negative on it.

Move the tracing paper around until the chosen area of the subject negative is projected in roughly the right place and then adjust the height of the enlarger until the size of the projected image is right. You may have to repeat this process a number of times before the image falls exactly right. It is possible to dispense with the tracing and make your adjustments on the background print itself but it is very difficult to see the projected image of the negative clearly against the detail of the print.

When the projected image is the right size, remove the tracing or print from the baseboard and make a number of prints from the negative—it is usually worth making two or three in case of mistakes while cutting. You do not need to print the entire negative, only the areas you want for montage. The prints are processed in the normal way but make sure the final wash is done

Title page *Even at its simplest, a cut and paste montage can convey a visual message that is not possible in a straight photograph*

Three of one *A very effective montage which combines several print images shot specially with this montage idea in mind*

thoroughly since any chemicals that remain on the prints may affect the glue used for montage work.

Place one of the finished prints on a cutting board and cut carefully round the chosen subject. Unless you want a very obvious looking result, you will need a sharp knife to cut the print—preferably a scalpel or a good craft knife. If you can afford it, try to use a new blade for cutting each print.

Once you have cut out the subject, place it on the background print and move it around until it is in the right position. While you are handling the prints, take care to keep them free from greasy finger marks or these will prevent a good bond later.

When you are satisfied with the positioning, place the tracing of the background over both prints and trace off the final position of the subject. The prints can then be prepared for pasting.

Apply a thin coating of suitable glue carefully to the back of the cut out subject and spread it out evenly, leaving a small gap around the very edge. Then, referring closely to the tracing, care-

Cut and paste montage

1 Select a suitable negative for the background and enlarge the image to your liking. Trace the image on white paper. This is later used for positioning

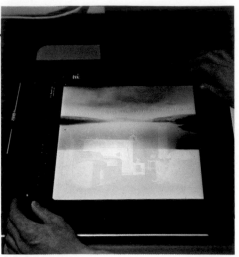

2 Print and process the background print and when it is dry place it on the easel. Line up and scale the second image by projecting it on the background print

3 The two prints necessary for the montage are shown, together with a glue stick, scalpel and a sandpaper stick which is used for paring the emulsion

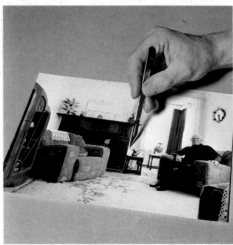

4 Lightly score the outline of the image to be removed. Make sure you cut only as deep as the emulsion layer. Use a new scalpel blade for each print

5 As excess paper is difficult to tear away without damaging the remaining areas, cut flaps. Concave areas are very difficult to remove otherwise

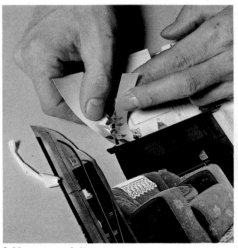

6 Very carefully tear away the excess areas of the print from the back of the remaining image. Firm, but not excessive pressure is needed for a neat job

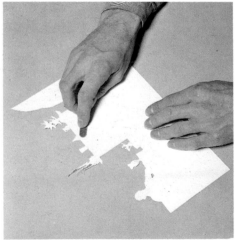

7 Sandpaper the edges of the print on the reverse side to remove paper fibres and to make the print wafer thin. Work from the centre outwards

8 Check the position and effect of the cut out image on the background print. For stability, mount the background print before adding the cut out image

9 Spread adhesive evenly over the back of the cut out image, taking particular care not to spoil the front of the print, or tear the delicate cutouts

fully place the cut out subject on the background, dropping it only when the positioning is just right. To bond it firmly, cover it with a clean sheet of paper to avoid finger marks, and press from the middle outwards. When the cut out seems to have stuck, carefully lift the paper and remove any excess glue. Leave the montage to dry properly and then add further images, if you want, following the same procedure.

These rough cut montages can be attractive and are very simple to make, but they are very obviously composite images; the thickness of the paper shows up the joins very clearly. If you want to disguise these, you must refine your technique a little.

Invisible joins
For invisible join montages, you have to be much more careful in your choice of images. The perspective, lighting angles, densities and other characteristics of the subject must closely match those in the background—otherwise the joins will stand out clearly no matter how good your technique. It is not always easy to judge the suitability of the images before you make the montage and at first it must be a matter of trial and error.

Once you have chosen your pictures, make a background print and prints for the images to be overlaid in exactly the same way as for rough cut montages. The difference comes in the cutting. Instead of cutting right through the print, you aim to merely lift off the top layer of the paper. This thin top layer is much less obvious when pasted on to the background.

Using a new knife blade for each print, cut away altogether the unwanted parts of the subject print leaving about 3 cm to spare around the outline of the subject. Then lightly score the front of the print exactly along the outline, cutting only just through the emulsion. Hold the print to the light to check that you have scored all the way around. Make a series of cuts right through the print outwards at right angles to the outline so that you make a series of small flaps—be careful not to stray over the scored line into the subject.

Place the print face down on a clean surface and bend it up gently around the subject area to crack the emulsion. Then, very carefully, tear away the unwanted areas, by pulling on each flap in turn. As each flap is pulled back, it will tear the backing paper away beneath the subject leaving just a thin layer of paper attached to the emulsion.

The final cutout for the subject is thus very thin at the edges where most of the paper backing is removed and it should blend almost imperceptibly into the background print. You can make the edges even thinner by placing the print face down and rubbing, from the centre outwards, with the finest grade of sandpaper, but beware of sanding it so thin that it is almost transparent, or detail from the background print may show.

This technique should work for all types of printing papers, though you may have some difficulty removing the backing from resin coated paper. If you do have difficulty, try to lift a corner of the backing with a sharp blade and then pull the corner firmly but evenly.

Once you have one thin overlay ready, paste it down following the same procedure as for rough cut montages, taking particular care over each step. Disguise the joins further by coating the whole montage with a matt spray—this also evens out the textures and the spray includes an ultraviolet screen that prevents print colours fading.

Copying
Unfortunately, invisible join montages may not last very long because the glue can affect the emulsion. So if you want a permanent image, it is worth making a copy by photographing the finished montage. The loss of quality inherent in copying is actually an advantage because it helps to disguise the joins even better. When lighting the montage for copying, make sure that any raised surfaces do not catch the light or throw obvious shadows.

Montage without glue
If you intend to make copies, it is not always necessary to paste the montage together. You can simply lay the cutout on top of the background and keep the montage flat under a sheet of glass. The completed montage can then be photographed. Glueless montage is less messy and allows you to use the various prints again, but it can be very difficult to keep the cutouts in place as you lay down the glass.

Whether you use rough cut, invisible join or glueless techniques, montage can allow you to create a wide range of pictorial effects ranging from complicated multiple images to fantastic surreal portraits and landscapes. Just a few are shown here and further possibilities are explored in a subsequent article. But the best way is to experiment.

Completed montage *After gluing, carefully position the cut out detail using the trace as a positioning guide, then place a heavy weight over the montage until dry*

Chapter 6
ADDING COLOUR
Hand colouring

Bikes *Hand colouring enables you to highlight areas with spectacular colour yet subdue other parts of a picture*

By hand colouring black and white prints you can create unique and distinctive pictures that fully express a personal, visual style. The procedure is straightforward—you apply dye or paint to a suitable print, using simple tools and working by normal light. The effects may be vivid or subtle, real or fantastic—much depends on your choice of pictorial subject and materials.

Hand colouring is not a substitute for colour printing, since the results are entirely different to those produced by ordinary colour printing. Nor should it be confused with retouching, which is usually done to correct mistakes or processing faults. Although many of the techniques of hand colouring are similar to those of retouching, the aim of hand colouring is to create an entirely new image based on a black and white original.

Choosing a print
The first requirement is a suitable print. Almost any black and white photograph can be hand coloured, but the subject matter and the way the image has been reproduced may affect your choice of materials. For example, it is usually easier to produce bright, vivid colours if you work with dyes, rather than oils, on fibre based papers. On the other hand, oil based colours make it easier to produce soft moody effects.

The best prints for hand colouring are generally rather flat and light, since dark tones tend to overwhelm the colours you apply. This is not an inflexible rule,

though. For example, a dark, contrasty print with a few brilliantly hand coloured highlights could be very effective with the right choice of subject.

For some hand coloured prints it is best to start with a sepia toned original if possible. Sepia toning gives you a softer and slightly more natural image tone to work on than the cold blacks and greys of a normal bromide print. This can be particularly effective if your picture includes skin tones. Alternatively, you could use a print made on a chloro-bromide paper such as Agfa Portriga, which also has a warm tone. You can also experiment with other types of toner that give different colours—the choice depends on your subject and your own tastes.

Paper choice is important. Although it is possible to colour both resin coated and fibre based papers, the best results usually come from fibre based prints. Resin coated paper tends to absorb water based dyes poorly, and oil based colours can only be used on fibre based paper. It is also better to avoid fibre-based paper which has a glossy, eggshell or any other unusual or shiny surface which might make it very hard to apply colour evenly. Matt or semi-matt surface papers are easiest to work with, as large areas of colour 'take' more easily—they are absorbed into the paper with less blotchiness.

Colouring materials and tools
There are two main kinds of colouring materials—water based and oil based. Water based colours include dyes, water colours and coloured inks. Oil based colours include artists oils, special photographic oils, and oil crayons. Dyes and inks are generally sold in bottles, either singly or in sets. Water colours and oils are most conveniently bought in sets, and are packaged in tubes. Oil crayons are soft, slightly oily sticks. Most of these materials can be bought at artists' suppliers. Photographic wetting agent, which can help water based colours flow on more evenly, is essential if you are attempting to colour resin coated prints.

Oil based colours have certain advantages for some photographs. Photographic oil colour can be easier to work with than water based colour, gives softer effects, and allows you to correct mistakes more easily. However, there is a tendency for the colours to spread out over the print when you even out the tones on large areas, so oils are generally more suitable for pictures with soft outlines and broad masses of tone rather than those which demand finely detailed colour work. You can use artists' oils to colour prints, but they need to be well diluted with a suitable medium and they do not have the same translucence as photographic oils.

Many other materials can be used to colour prints. Only experiment will tell you whether or not a particular paint or dye works on your pictures. Many types of food dye, for example, can be used successfully.

To be on the safe side, though, you should make your first experiments with colours sold specifically for photographic use. Most paints and inks take their colour from suspended particles of pigment. These fine particles—and the gum used to bind them to the paper—may remain visible on the surface of the print. If you find this objectionable, then you should use dyes which are completely soluble and are absorbed into the print emulsion. A further advantage of photographic retouching dyes is that they are reproduced on film just as they are seen by the eye. This is useful if you want to make exact copies.

Cotton wool swabs and artists' paint brushes are usually used to apply colour to a print. The best sable brushes are expensive, but last well if looked after. But if you only intend to hand colour prints infrequently it is far more economical to buy camel, squirrel or ox hair types. Always clean your brushes thoroughly after use, form the hairs into their working shape, then lie them flat and leave them to dry in the air. A range of sizes from a very fine 00 (which can also be used for print spotting) up to a size 6 should cover most of your needs. Choose softer hair brushes for water based colour work and stiffer types for oil work.

Cotton wool, absorbent paper, masking tape, a water jar and some old saucers to use as palettes will also be needed.

You should work in good light on a large surface such as a plastic or glass covered table. Daylight is best for judging colours. Try out your colours first on a spare print of the one you intend working on.

Using water based colour

For your first experiments with hand colouring it is probably easiest to use photographic retouching dyes. The principles for using dyes, though, are very similar for all water based mediums.

If large areas of the print are to be coloured, soak it first in water. This will allow the dye to spread evenly and soak well into the paper. If you only wish to colour small areas of a print you need not

Woodland puddle *A small patch of blue offsets the subtle colours used to enhance this picture*

soak it first. When the print is thoroughly wet, remove it from the water and sponge or squeegee any surface droplets off the print. To prevent the print from curling as it dries, and to hold it in place while you work, tape the edges of the print down to your work surfaces. Use masking tape or gummed paper tape.

It is best to work with very dilute dyes

and build up layers of colour gradually. If your colour is too strong, there is more chance of producing a blotchy result. Add concentrated dye drop by drop to a small quantity of water in a saucer until you have a weak dye solution.

Colour large areas first using cotton wool swabs dipped in the dye solution. Go over the area with repeated applications of dye until the colour is as strong as you want it. Work quickly so that the print does not dry out before you have completed the large even toned areas such as the sky. This is more likely to happen if you use RC paper, since only a small amount of water is absorbed by the emulsion layer of the print. With fibre based paper, the absorbent base material acts as a reservoir and keeps the print damp. Use a gentle circular rubbing motion. Colours can be given subtle gradation by adding a touch of a darker colour dye to subsequent applications. A slightly darker blue can be applied to the upper part of a sky, for instance.

If you need to cover two adjacent areas of even tone with different colours,

Girl in helmet *Even conventional colour photography cannot match the subtlety of hand applied colours*

Toning and colouring procedures

1 *To hand colour a print, you need colour paint or dyes—special photo dyes are best—a few brushes, some blotting paper and a sponge*

2 *Soak a fibre based print in water before commencing large scale hand colouring. Small pinpoints of colour may be added to a dry print*

3 *A sepia toned print gives a softer and more natural image to work on. Start by bleaching the print in the solution provided with the toner*

4 *When the image has bleached as far as it will go, wash the print thoroughly, then swab it with toner (hydrogen sulphide) to restore the image*

5 *If you need to cover adjacent areas with different colours, or wish to protect areas from accidental colouring, apply masking lacquer to the dry print*

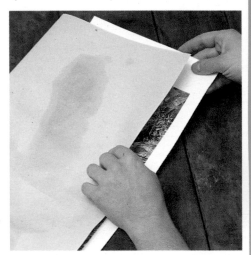

6 *After soaking the print for at least five minutes, dry it carefully between folds of absorbent paper, so it remains damp to the touch*

7 *Try out the colours you intend using on a spare print—a test print is ideal for this. Strong colours should be diluted before use*

8 *Carefully work over the larger areas you intend colouring, using successive 'washes' of dilute colour to build up colour strength gradually*

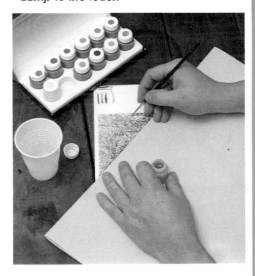

9 *Localized colour is applied using fine brushes. Brush off each colour to check colour match. Protect coloured areas with absorbent paper*

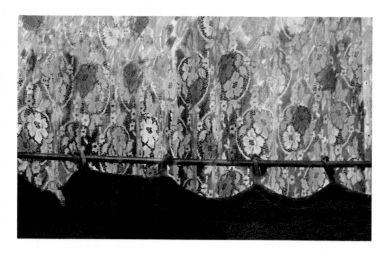

you may have problems with the colours bleeding into each other where they meet. One way to solve this problem is to mask off areas of the print with rubber-based masking lacquer (available from art suppliers), or water-diluted latex based glue that can be peeled off the print after use. After you have coloured one area, allow the print to dry and then cover the coloured area with masking lacquer. The print can then be resoaked without any risk of the dye washing out or spreading, and you can set to work on the rest of the image.

Once you have coloured all the larger areas of the print, you can work on the fine details. Use brushes for these small parts of the image.

You should work slowly and carefully to obtain the best effect. As you gain experience with the technique, you can expect to take more, rather than less time to complete a print. If you should make a mistake while colouring a print, you may be able to rescue the print by giving it a long soak in running water to remove most of the dye. Do not expect this to work every time, though, it is better to regard the dyes that you paint on to your prints as permanent. As another precaution against errors, and as a matter of good style, you should try to start with the paler colours and work up to the more intense bright colours. This gives you more control and makes it easier to visualize the finished effect.

Because dye can be difficult to remove from your skin, you should wear gloves when you colour prints, particularly if you apply the colour with hand-held cotton wool swabs.

Using oil based colour

As with water based colours, it is possible to use a variety of types of oil colours, but the best results are usually given by using colours specially made for tinting photographs. These are more translucent than ordinary oil paints and have a consistency that makes them more suitable for applying to photographs.

Oils are usually applied thinly, like a stain on the surface of the print, rather than in built up layers like a conventional painting.

Ideally, prints to be coloured with oils should be properly mounted before you begin work to prevent curling or

Fabric *Spots of intense colour accentuate the design of the fabric in this picture.*
Vase of flowers *You can use a printed image as a base to create a kind of 'painting'*

damage to the edges and corners. However, it is usually sufficient simply to tape the print to your work surface. Prints should not be dampened before you apply the colour.

Mix small quantities of the required colour on your palette, adding a little turpentine if you need to thin the paint down. The colour can be applied to large areas with either brushes or cotton wool. The special virtue of oil based colour is that it can be pushed around the surface of fibre based prints to even out tones. This is not possible with water based colours, which tend to be absorbed into the print emulsion as soon as they are applied. If you apply

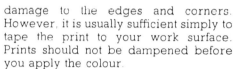

colour unevenly, you can spread it around by rubbing with a piece of cotton wool, or even your finger, until the tones are evenly distributed. You can blend different colours together on the surface of the print with the same technique. If this soft effect is not wanted, then you must allow each area of colour to dry before applying colour to an adjacent area. When thinly applied, photo oils do not take as long to dry as conventionally applied artists oils, but the drying process takes long enough to make colouring of sharp edged adjacent details a relatively lengthy procedure.

A particular advantage of oil-based colour is that mistakes can usually be removed with a piece of cotton wool dipped in turpentine.

Some oil based crayons and pastels can also be used for colouring photographs. The pastels are simply applied to a dry print, and then blended in afterwards using a pad of cotton wool moistened with a mixture of thinner and oil medium.

If you wish to combine water based dyes and oil based colours, you should start by applying the dyes to a wet print. When the print is dry, you can move on to applying the oil based colours. Tiny pin-points of colour, whatever the medium, should be applied last of all.

The basic techniques of hand colouring photographs allow you to produce truly individual pictures that reflect your own taste and pictorial style. Once you become confident with the basic methods, you can try a more advanced technique, air brushing.

Portrait *Hand coloured black and white prints are well suited to subjects like portraiture where a particular period effect is required*

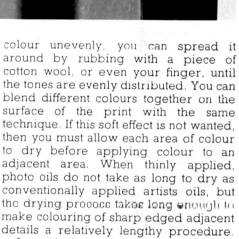

Airbrush techniques

An airbrush is a very small, fine and precise spray gun, the size of a heavy pen, which you can use to apply areas of tone or colour to a print to eliminate compositional mistakes or to change the colour or tone density of certain areas.

Compressed air from either a sealed can or, alternatively, from a motor powered compressor, propels liquid through the airbrush nozzle to project a fine spray rather like a conventional spray gun. The difference between a spray gun and an airbrush, however, is that the nature of the spray from the airbrush can be finely controlled. By adjusting the air pressure, the paint supply and method of application you can use an airbrush to accurately colour-match existing print colours, and perfectly retouch any image. The spray can be a heavy 'spatter' or a fine mist over a wide or narrow area.

You will often need a conventional brush to retouch small details, such as hairlines and spots, but by using the airbrush corrections to large areas of the print can be almost invisible—but, it must be said, only with considerable practice. Always have several copies of your chosen print available for practice and experimentation: mistakes and mis-calculations frequently occur.

The main photographic use of an airbrush is to improve the evenness of tone of an image, or to bring up one tone in relation to another. It is also used for covering up any blemishes which may be due to faulty or dirty negatives, uneven development (of print or neg.) or poor enlarging equipment. Haze can be introduced into areas of the print to 'distance' sharp backgrounds.

An airbrush is very effective for introducing or emphasizing highlights and shadows to tidy up and brighten an image. These can be often outside the density range of the print, and skilfully employed can give the picture a super-real quality.

Special effects, such as the invisible joining of images on multiple prints or removing backgrounds, are easily accomplished with an airbrush. You can create false information such as the addition of clouds with practice. And you can add colour to black and white prints: in extreme cases, you can even rework an image or a subject which is unsharp, too flat, or lacking in impact and detail. Advertising still life photographs, are often completely retouched in this way. 'Cut-aways', such as the insides of car engines, are often combinations of pure photographs and airbrush retouching. So too are many of the dramatic cloudy skies in the background.

Preparations

It is important to see well when airbrushing, so work in good light. Use a bright striplight, or an adjustable lamp balanced for colour work. It is best to sit on a stool and tilt the print towards you.

Apart from the airbrush and colour mixing equipment (see below), you will need card or proprietary materials for masking, masking tape, a scalpel, and a magnifying glass for fine work. Most art shops now have special sections which deal only with airbrush accessories. You

Snake charmer *Airbrushing is often used to create surreal images, simply because airbrush effects can look so real*

Aerial warfare *Airbrushing can be a very effective way of removing unwanted detail from a print—here, an unsightly television aerial on the roof of the old inn has been neatly eliminated. Providing the print is properly masked during airbrushing and colours are carefully matched, the traces of such subterfuge are difficult to spot (below right)*

Adding colour *A black and white image (above) subtly and delicately retouched in colour with an airbrush*

Airbrush construction

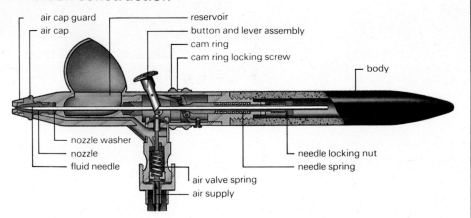

air cap guard
air cap
reservoir
button and lever assembly
cam ring
cam ring locking screw
body
nozzle washer
nozzle
fluid needle
needle locking nut
needle spring
air valve spring
air supply

Airbrush operation

An airbrush is similar in appearance to a fat fountain pen, but in place of the nib there is a nozzle-set through which a fine spray of colour or tone is propelled by compressed air.

Behind the spray nozzle is a small recessed reservoir for the colour, and behind that the control button. Directly below the control button, which points upwards, is the connection for the compressed air lead, on a screw thread.

The control button controls both the air valve (and hence the air pressure), and the position of the needle, which runs right through the airbrush, ending in an extremely fine point which rests in the nozzle. The exact fitting of the needle and its nozzle, the 'nozzle-set', controls the spray.

The needle passes through the colour reservoir then to the nozzle. The air valve below the button and nozzle-set normally remains closed when the brush is not in use.

You should hold the airbrush lightly in your hand, like a pencil, positioning the control button so the tip of your forefinger rests over it. Your second or third finger should rest against the air lead below, helping to steady the airbrush and keep it upright.

Angle the airbrush at 45° to the surface of your print when working normally, and pass the airlead over the back of your hand and away from the work.

With the airbrush receiving air at the correct pressure, and with colour in the reservoir, gently press down on the button to activate the flow of compressed air through the air cap, at the tip of the airbrush, which surrounds and protects the nozzle-set. No colour emerges from the airbrush until you begin to draw back the button towards your wrist.

The passage of air in the air cap forms a slight vacuum at the tip of the nozzle set, and as you draw back the needle, the colour is sucked from the tip, and atomized into a fine spray.

The further you draw back the button, the greater the flow of colour. When you have finished the work, let the button run forward to cut off the flow of colour, before you release the downward (air supply) pressure. If you do not follow this procedure, liquid colour will be left on the needle tip and will escape as a blot or blob when you next start work.

It is essential to keep the same downward pressure on the button throughout. If the air supply is not maintained at a constant pressure, the texture of spray tone will be uneven. As the pressure drops the texture becomes coarser. If you set the air pressure correctly, you should be able to balance exactly the grain and texture of the original.

To repeat work of a particular colour density you can set the colour flow at a constant rate by setting the cam ring, which is situated behind the control button. Undo the cam ring locking screw then turn the ring clockwise to draw the needle away from its nozzle. Lock the ring when you have reached the required volume. With this method a set amount of colour is released just by pressing down on the button, but you can still release more colour by pulling back the button further.

You need a constant supply of compressed air to operate the airbrush. This air must be clean, free from dust and grit, and free from oil or water vapour.

Small electric compressors, with reservoir, valve and air filters are now quite cheap, but tins of 'liquid' air are becoming increasingly popular.

Common spray faults

a) Airbrush texture too coarse: increase the air pressure.

b) Uneven broken-line spray: the pigment is probably too coarse. Remix the colour and wash out the airbrush.

c) Spray heavier one side than another: there is a blockage in the air cap.

d) Colour leaking from nozzle with the needle closed: colour has dried in the nozzle, remove it and soak it in solvent.

e) Colour splatter or spitting: failure to depress the button *first* to release the air.

Retouching with an airbrush

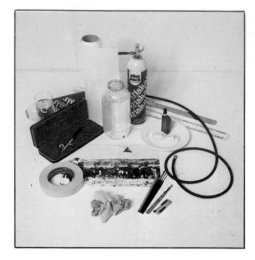

1 *Basic airbrushing equipment consists of: airbrush, compressed air, suitable inks, masking tape and film, and mixing, cutting and cleaning utensils*

2 *Always practise brushing techniques beforehand to ensure everything is in correct working order. Practise, too, the brushing strokes you will be using*

3 *Some form of masking is nearly always needed to protect parts of the image from spray. Cut masks large enough to cover the print and its mount*

7 *When the previous application has dried, you can spray on the base coat in a tone which matches the rest of the print. This acts as the base for fine detail*

8 *Add fine detail gradually, allowing each coat to dry before applying the next. Practise on unwanted prints until you are sure of your technique and the effect*

9 *When the final coat has dried, carefully peel back the masking film and discard it. Remove the print from its backing if a temporary mount has been used*

will also need cotton wool buds, and sable brushes Nos. 1, 2 and 3 for spotting and finishing off fine detail.

All prints must be taped flat or dry or spray-mounted before airbrushing on a hard, flat surface. Grease marks on prints, particularly fingermarks, will show up as definite textures under air-brush detail so, after mounting, clean your print with a weak solution of ammonia to degrease it.

Using an airbrush
Before you start work on any print, thoroughly familiarize yourself with the operation of the brush (see panel) and practise getting the effects you want on pieces of blank card.

The spray liquid in the reservoir is always called *colour* whether it is intended for black and white re-touching, or coloured for colour work You can use black or white paint, water based artists colours, oil colours, and spirit dyes—indeed anything thin enough to be sprayed easily. But the colour must be free from any grit that may block the nozzle-set of the brush.

Avoid colours which dry and cake easily, these clog the airbrush. It is best to buy tubes of specially manufactured air-brush colours which are easy to dilute to the correct consistency with clean water. Remember to replace tops of tubes or pots immediately after use.

Connect the flexible lead first to the air supply, then turn on the supply to blow out any dust in the hose. Then attach the lead to your airbrush. You need to set the air pressure differently depending on the type of colour you use. Follow the manufacturer's instructions for any particular type of colour. In general, spirit colours need less pressure than oil-based or *gouache* (thick, opaque water colour) paints. There is no advantage in setting the pressure too high, and too much air will dislodge stencil films, if you use them on the work.

You can use an airbrush to retouch either colour or black and white prints. With black and white prints, you simply use a mixture of white and black dyes to give a grey of the right shade to eliminate unwanted details. With black dye in the airbrush, you can strengthen shadows in a

black and white print—prints often suffer from imperfectly black shadows.

For colour prints, the technique is usually to spray the unwanted detail or area with process white before building it up again in the desired colour. If you spray the colour straight on without the white base layer, the colours underneath will tend to show through, giving a mixture—though of course, you can often use this mix creatively, spraying blue paint over yellow to produce green.

Mix gouache colour on a clean palette using a round hoghair brush (No. 5 or 6). Use turpentine to dilute oil colours, or clean water for water colours. You need only dilute the colour sufficiently to allow it to flow evenly in the airbrush—it should just drip off the loading brush. You can spray delicate tints from a full strength colour in the reservoir by adjusting the nozzle for a very fine spray.

To obtain detail on the photograph, you must first use a *body* colour, a mix of white and the colour in use. To change the colour of the image, spray only with a pure colour mix. Holding the airbrush at the correct angle as recommended by

4 *With a new scalpel blade, cut through the mask—but be careful not to damage the print below. Cut into areas of dark detail to avoid a 'halo' effect*

5 *Carefully peel back the mask film from the area to be worked. This can be discarded or reapplied for subsequent work in other areas of the image*

6 *If, as here, you are removing detail from a photograph, begin by spraying suitable opaque over it to match the colour of the surrounding area*

10 *Some retouching with a brush may still be necessary—particularly if you wish to add fine detail which is beyond the scope of an airbrush*

Chopped chopper *The helicopter in this shot (above) spoils the authentic 'ranching' feel which is presented quite effectively in the rest of the photograph, and the sky is rather flat and featureless. Below, the same shot with the helicopter airbrushed out and detail added to the sky to strengthen the image*

the manufacturer, load the airbrush by wiping the hoghair brush downwards into the reservoir, until two-thirds full.

Operate the control button as described in the panel, and practise making strokes on a sheet of scrap paper, stopping the colour flow only at the end of each stroke, while keeping the button depressed to continue the release of air. Always move the nozzle of the brush smoothly and parallel to the surface to give an even distribution of colour—simply swinging the brush from side to side gives an even spray tapering out at either end of the swing.

To build up tints, overlap each stroke by half so that the coverage is even. For solid colour application the airbrush should be about ten centimetres from the work. The airbrush sprays out a cone of colour, and the nearer you work to the print the sharper the spray line will become. Practice will make this obvious.

You can use the airbrush for fine line work. Adjust the nozzle to a fine jet and spray the work, at a suitable angle, allowing the air to escape freely over and across the paper surface.

Montage *Air-brushing is used extensively in advertising to create 'impossible' images which may or may not stem from single images. Here, three originals were combined in stages to give the image at left. This was then airbrushed to add and tidy detail*

flat on the print will result in a sharp edge, but if you hold the card away from the surface of the print, the result will be a soft edge known as unsharp masking.

The most advanced masking technique involves using a special transparent, slightly adhesive film, which is protected by a backing paper, readily available from art shops. Cut a sheet of the film to the full image size and peel off the backing paper and then carefully place the tacky film down on to the image, expelling air bubbles. Using a scalpel with a new blade, carefully score the film, *but not the print,* along the required image outline. Peel away the film from the image area on to which you intend to spray, then complete your airbrushing. The advantage of this type of masking is that you can replace the cut away film to protect your first area should you wish to colour the rest of the image differently. Be very careful to avoid stretching the film when peeling it from the print. Again this technique needs practice.

Preserving an airbrushed image

Airbrushed images are very delicate and are easily smudged or damaged with rough treatment. Indeed, if your results are unsatisfactory, you can remove all the airbrush work (except colour-dye work) by washing it off quickly with cotton wool soaked in a suitable solvent.

To preserve a particular effect, copy your result on to a suitable film type using your camera or enlarger. Or you can protect a finished print by filling the airbrush with a solution of clear gum arabic and evenly spraying the whole print. Alternatively, use a proprietary matt or gloss print spray, which also includes an ultraviolet fade-resistant coating. Spraying the print also helps to make airbrushed areas indistinguishable from original print areas, as it unifies the surface texture. Like all valuable photographs, you should protect an airbrushed print with a sheet of clean paper or tissue.

Always be sparing in your use of colour because if you release too much, you may flood the work with liquid colour, and splatter it in all directions. Build up colour by repeated applications rather than in one heavy coat. To spray a graduated tint, start close to the work with a dense band of colour and pull the brush back, working away from it. Raise the airbrush at each stroke and as you work move away from the dense edge. In this way you can build up a tint which changes in density from dark to light yet shows no hard lines in the transition.

Stencils and masks

In order to stop colour spreading to areas where it is not wanted you will nearly always need to mask your photograph as you airbrush it. Even the most experienced worker, when spraying fine details and retouching close to the print, uses masks to keep the rest of the image clean, and clear of colour drift.

The simplest masks involve taping down strips of thin card with removable masking tape that does not leave a sticky mark on the print. You can use masks for sharp or unsharp masking. Card which is

Chapter 7
NEW VIEWS
Tricks and illusions

Distorted images, unusual colour combinations, ghost images and false perspective—all these are photographic 'tricks', which you can do with almost any camera, and without any special equipment. By using a variety of simple techniques, you can obtain some startlingly unreal effects.

Using various coloured filters, for instance, you can make multiple exposures on colour film, giving unreal colours to certain parts of a moving image. You can also use the flare caused by out of focus reflected light to your own advantage, giving whatever shape you wish to the reflections. Both transparent and reflective surfaces can be used to make distorted or 'ghost'

images in a variety of ways, while the *linear shutter* technique allows you to create striking images distorted in one direction only, giving an exaggerated illusion of speed. You can also falsify perspective to give out of scale effects, and change the apparent relative sizes of objects in a photograph.

All these techniques are rather unpredictable, and often a small change can produce radically different results. However, since you are experimenting, there is no such thing as getting a shot 'wrong'—you simply achieve the effect you want by trial and error. While this may mean using large quantities of film to achieve a given effect, you might also get an unexpectedly attractive result.

Colour movement
If you make three exposures of a moving object on the same frame of colour negative film, using a different coloured filter each time, each image of the object appears in a different colour. Where the images overlap, they show combinations of the colours of the filters used.

Any subject with a certain amount of movement is suitable—running water, clouds, washing flapping in the breeze—but a subject with bright highlights or white areas gives the most scope. The

Surreal sea *By making three multiple exposures through blue, green and red filters, moving subjects can be made to take on bright, fantastic colours*

effect is more interesting if parts of the subject are stationary, because if you use the right combination of filters the stationary parts of the subject are reproduced in their natural colours, while the moving parts show as separate, differently coloured images. For example, a person sitting in front of a fountain photographed in this way would appear in natural colours, while the moving water would be split into an infinite number of different hues. For this technique, the camera must be firmly fixed, to ensure that the three exposures are all in register.

The three filters must be in the primary colours, red, blue and green. You may be able to buy normal photographic filters in these colours. Otherwise, you must buy filters designed for making colour separations in the darkroom. These sometimes come in large sheets which must be cut down to size. You can either tape them to the front of the lens barrel or cut them precisely to fit a filter holder. Suitable filter sets would

Distorted flower *Textured glass and plastic material can be used to break up an image of a familiar object into a brightly coloured abstract pattern*

be Kodak Wratten no. 25 (red) no. 61 (green) and no. 38A (blue).

To make the necessary exposures, set the camera firmly upon a tripod and make a multiple exposure in three parts—that is, three exposures on the same frame. For each of the three exposures you must use a different one of the three filters. The order in which you use the filters does not affect the success of the technique and you can alter it freely.

Exposure should be established by experiment, but as a rough guide, take a reflected light reading from the subject —without a filter on the lens if you are using a TTL meter—increase the indicated exposure by one stop, and give that exposure through each filter. It is not advisable to take readings with a filter on the lens since the meter is affected differently by different colours —a red filter especially can make a meter under-read by up to half a stop. To increase your chances of success, it is

best to bracket exposures when using this technique.

Colour negative film is most suited to this kind of special effect, because reversal film has a smaller exposure latitude. Colour negative film also allows you to correct the colour balance of the stationary parts of the subject at the printing stage. It is advisable, too, to use a lens hood, as filters can cause a large amount of unwanted flare.

Masks for highlights
When you look at bright highlights or reflections which are out of focus, they appear as bright discs in the viewfinder. These discs are the image of the lens opening or the diaphragm—the more out of focus the wider the aperture and the longer the lens, the bigger they appear. If, for example, you point a long telephoto lens at a sheet of water catching the sun, the entire picture consists of bright circles. If you keep the image out of focus but stop the lens down, the reflections take on the shape of the

diaphragm itself—usually a hexagon. You can achieve the same effect by cutting out a mask in any shape you like, from black card, and placing it in front of the lens, either by wedging it behind a UV filter or by sandwiching it between two filters which you then screw into the lens. Alternatively, you could slide the mask into the mount used for slide-in plastic filters.

The reflections assume whatever shape you cut out of the mask, and the scope for experiment is considerable. You can, for example, use the reflections found in nature—solar reflections off water or shiny surfaces—but you can just as well make your own, indoors. By placing a background at a sufficient distance from an object and then defocusing it, you can make the object stand out against a pattern of stars, crescents or any other shapes you choose.

One way to obtain this effect is to set up a dark background made of card or

cloth punctured with small holes, and to light it from behind, either with a lamp or with electronic flash. It is best, however, to have a continuous light source. Another way is to use crumpled foil lit from in front, and sufficiently out of focus for only the highlights to register.

These effects are most suitable for still life shots or portraits, where you want a special atmosphere.

You can also colour the shapes by using coloured lights, or even by making several exposures of the background alone, with different coloured filters fitted over the lens. By shooting the main subject reflected in a mirror on which you have glued small pieces of silver foil, you can make the bright out of focus shapes appear in front of the main part of the subject.

Image distortion
You can deliberately distort images in a number of ways, and although it is often difficult to control distortion, it can give interesting results.

Uneven glass The most obvious means of obtaining a distorted image is to photograph through a transparent substance of uneven thickness such as various types of glass or plastic panels and windows with patterns in relief. The variety of possible effects is considerable —as you move the camera and shoot from a different angle, the image becomes twisted or compressed into unrecognisable shapes. By excluding anything which gives the illusion away, you can obtain weird and often attractive distorted images.

It is best to use an SLR for this kind of effect, because the smallest change of angle makes a great difference, and since you often have to shoot quite close to the glass, the viewfinder of a non-reflex camera can be misleading. Remember, too, to focus on the image behind the glass, not on the glass itself.

With some kinds of hammered glass or moulded plastic, the subject is broken up into fragments, but remains recognizable in outline and colour, usually when it is very close to the glass. In this case, you can focus on the glass itself, and position the camera directly facing the subject rather than at an angle. By backlighting the subject you could obtain a fragmented silhouette, and if you shoot through coloured glass, an attractive coloured silhouette effect can be obtained.

Water baths Another way of distorting some small subjects—even a photographic print—is to place them in a shallow tray of water such as a developing dish, positioning the camera directly overhead. By ruffling the water surface or agitating the dish you can distort the image in various ways. Again, you should focus on the image, not on the water surface above it.

This technique is best suited to photographic images or lettering, but you could experiment with any flat image. It is important to ensure that the paper stays below the surface—resin-coated paper tends to float, so you should

weight it at the corners, with coins for example. For large paper sizes, fibre based paper is preferable.

Remember that the water surface can show a reflection of the camera itself, so avoid this by adjusting the lighting carefully. If you use flash, the image will be sharp and clear, while by artificial light or daylight you can use slow shutter speeds, and blur the image. **Reflected images** Any reflection is a distortion of the original image if the reflecting surface is not completely flat, and you can use this principle in a number of ways to produce distorted images.

Images reflected in water are distorted by the slightest ripple—much less than is required to distort an underwater image. To photograph a reflection in water, set up the subject and the water surface in reflection-free surroundings, such as a darkened room. Arrange the lighting to light the subject only, not the water, and focus on the reflected image, not the water surface. Again, by excluding all tell-tale signs from the picture, you can achieve completely unreal effects.

Similar effects can be produced using solid reflecting surfaces—you can use a highly polished print glazing sheet as a distorting mirror, or even the magnifying side of a shaving mirror. With the former, you can control the image by bending the sheet as required, and

Starry eyed If background highlights are out of focus, they form round discs of light on the film. But by putting a card mask over the lens, the shape of the highlights can be varied at will

securing it in position with adhesive tape, while with a shaving mirror you must adjust the angle of the camera in relation to the mirror's surface.

With most mirrors, you obtain a secondary image, caused by the layer of glass which covers the actual reflecting surface. Front-surfaced mirrors, like those used on SLRs, can be used, but they are fragile and expensive. With a metal sheet such as a print glazing sheet, this secondary image does not appear, because the image is reflected directly from the surface.

Ghost images

By using a special semi-silvered mirror, you can produce 'ghost' images. This type of mirror, also known as a 'two way' mirror, is only partly coated with reflecting material, evenly distributed all over its surface. If an object placed behind it is sufficiently illuminated, it is visible as well as the reflected image, and can appear to be part of it. Since this type of mirror is used for interior decor, it is available in a variety of sizes.

Ghost image shots are most easily done indoors. Set up the camera and the subject in front of the reflecting side of the mirror, so that the subject is visible in the viewfinder. The camera and subject must be opposite each other, at the same angle to the mirror's surface and at the same distance, if possible. Position the second subject behind the mirror, so that the two images coincide. Remember to focus on the images rather that the glass surface.

The lighting for the second subject depends on the reflection rating of the mirror, but almost always has to be stronger than that for the reflected subject. Adjust the lighting for the balance you require, bearing in mind that the contrast of the image as seen in the viewfinder is less than that you obtain on the film.

It is important to light only the portions of the subjects you want to reproduce—or you might find that unwanted elements of background intrude on the picture and conflict with each other. Alter the lighting to suit the effect you want—the scope is tremendous.

Figure in a bottle You can photograph a figure 'in' a bottle using this technique. The bottle must be larger and therefore closer to the mirror, but it does not matter if it is in front of the mirror or behind it. Light the bottle in such a way that a dark space is left in the middle, where the figure will be. This is not difficult, because glassware is easily lit as an outline.

Place the person in such a position that they appear to be in the bottle when viewed through the viewfinder. The figure should be set against a dark background that does not intrude and

Reflected landscape *Distortion is made possible by using reflectors. Here a piece of flexible plastic mirror is being used to add a new twist to landscape*

Linear shutter *A special slitscan camera was used to shoot this distorted image, but even with a simple camera and a few very simple techniques, you can easily take similar pictures*

destroy the illusion. If the bottle's background is included, it must be definite enough not to appear as a ghost image.

Since the bottle and the figure are at different distances from the mirror, use the smallest aperture possible, to obtain maximum depth of field—it may even be necessary to use a wide angle lens to ensure that both bottle and figure are in focus. With this effect as with others, the only way to achieve the result you want is trial and error.

You can sometimes produce the same

illusion using a sheet of normal glass— here, too, the effect you produce depends on the relative strengths of the lighting used on the different elements in the shot. With either method, take care to eliminate extraneous reflections from the glass itself, which can obscure the parts you want to photograph completely.

Linear shutters

Even more dramatic distortions of moving subjects can be achieved using a linear shutter. This attachment, which

fits over the front of the lens, consists of a mask with only a narrow slit which lets in light. As the exposure is made, the film is wound back manually through the camera, and the subject, recorded only through the narrow slit, is grotesquely lengthened or shortened in the direction of the film movement.

To use this device, first fit a wide angle lens such as a 24 mm or a 28 mm. With the cap over the lens, wind on and release the shutter until the film is completely wound on the take-up spool, as if it had been completely exposed. Place the camera on a tripod, and, removing the lens cap, fit the linear shutter on the front of the lens. Set the

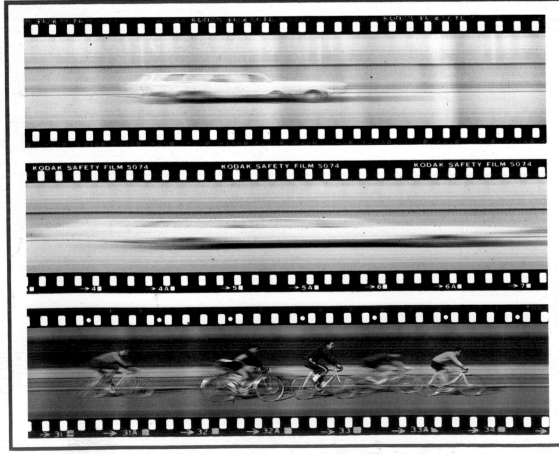

Movement and distortion

The major problem with the slitscan technique is matching the speed of the subject to the film rewind speed. Failure to match them results in a distorted image. Also, vertical strips of uneven exposure are caused by jerky film wind. The top picture was taken by hand-winding the film as the car drove past at 35 mph. The shape is recognizable, but unevenly exposed. When the power rewind on the camera's motor drive was used to eliminate any unevenness, the outline of the car was stretched out of shape. **Results like those in the lower** picture require plenty of practice. It is probably better to start with black and white film, as this allows you to see the results very quickly, and then move on to colour as your skill and confidence increase.

Perspective effects

Because a photograph is a two-dimensional representation of a three-dimensional subject, the viewer relies heavily on the impression of perspective to perceive the illusion of depth in the picture. By interfering with the way perspective is recorded in a photograph, you can create out of scale effects such as, for example, a figure apparently standing on a hand, but actually much further from the camera than the hand.

To do this it is essential to remove all elements in the picture which give clues to distance—without making the remaining elements look like cut-outs. The hand itself can conceal what is supporting the person. It is important to use lighting of the same type for both the figure and the hand to make it look as if they are both lit by the same light source. The ideal background to such a shot is a plain one such as a blank wall.

Often, the illusion is helped when the two elements are at some distance from the camera, especially as this helps you obtain good depth of field. A distant viewpoint compresses the apparent distance between objects, thus helping produce the illusion. Try selecting a low camera angle, as this, too, tends to falsify perspective. Carefully falsifying visual clues to depth in photographs such as the way texture becomes finer in the distance, can give some weird illusions.

Sun trap *Some of the most spectacular effects are very simple to achieve. This perspective trick was just a matter of the right camera angle*

camera shutter on B, and lock it open with a cable release. Press the rewind release catch on the camera, and, as the subject moves past the camera, rewind the film several turns back into the cassette. When you have made the exposures you want in this fashion, you can unlock the shutter release button, finish winding the film back into the cassette, and develop it normally.

When rewinding the film, try to do this as smoothly as possible—ideally, a slow electric motor should be used. The relation between the subject movement and the film movement determines distortion. If, for example, you rewind the film rapidly and the subject is moving across the frame in the opposite direction, it will be elongated; if it moves in the same direction as the film, it will be compressed.

With experience, you can learn to 'follow' the subject, and, depending on the irregularity of the movement, produce the most strange and unexpected results on the film.

Exposure when using a linear shutter is also a matter of trial and error, since the light reaching the film through the slit in the shutter is governed by the speed at which the film is rewound. However, as a rough guide, set the lens to a medium aperture, such as $f/8$, in bright sunlight.

Panoramas

If you have ever tried to capture on a photograph the dramatic sweep of a distant landscape, you will know how frustrating it can be. A wide angle lens is most suitable for showing the breadth and scale of the scene, but tends to result in large expanses of foreground and sky. A standard or telephoto lens, however, is better for picking out detail, but only takes in a narrow view.

A useful way to get around the dilemma of which lens to use is to shoot a panorama—take a series of photographs from the same viewpoint, but pan the camera a little between each exposure. The prints of these pictures are then joined up to form a continuous strip, so that the entire image conveys something of the grandeur of the view, yet still retains all the interesting detail.

To get the best from a panorama, choose your viewpoint and subject carefully. If possible, try to avoid scenes where everything is very distant, or there will not be any variation in scale in the final picture. A better choice is a scene where the important elements vary in size, or are at a range of distances from the camera, so that they do not appear a uniform scale in the print. Take care, though, that nothing is so big or so close to the camera that it obscures important detail in the distance.

Continuous tone areas are difficult to join successfully, whereas subjects with many clearly defined lines make the process of marrying up the various elements much easier. For this reason, clear blue skies or wide expanses of water are best avoided. A sky broken up by small puffy clouds is much more suitable, as is a landscape crisscrossed by roads, buildings, hedges or walls.

Static subjects are easiest to shoot, but where there are moving figures or vehicles visible, these can actually be used to add interest to the picture, provided that they are fairly central in each of the images that make up the panorama. If there is movement near the edges, there is a danger that there will be difficulties in joining up the final image. Confining movement to the centre of the frame eliminates this.

Once you have chosen your viewpoint, you can begin to set up your tripod and camera in preparation for the pictures. Although hand-held panoramas are possible, a tripod makes life a lot easier. Besides eliminating camera shake, it allows you to use a smaller aperture for better definition and depth of field, and ensures that the horizon remains at the same level within the frame in each consecutive picture.

London panorama *By panning the camera between exposures, you can take in a broad view, even with a standard lens. You must make sure that the camera is level, however, or the horizon will curve—as it does in this picture*

This last requirement can only be satisfied, however, if the tripod has a pan and tilt head, and is correctly levelled. To level the tripod, set all the adjustments to zero—there is generally a marker on each movement—and place a spirit level on the top plate. Make sure that the bubble tube is at right angles to one of the three legs, then adjust the remaining two legs. When the bubble is central within the tube, turn the level through 90°, and level the bubble again, but this time use only the third leg. If you follow this procedure, you should be able to level the tripod quite quickly, and with the minimum of fuss.

Next attach the camera, and check that as you pan across the scene, the horizon does not appear to move up or down the frame. If it does, it may well be that the

Himalayan mountainscape *If you do not have a wide angle lens, a panoramic picture may be the only way to capture the grandeur of a scene. To conceal the joins in this picture, a red filter was used to turn the sky black*

tripod head is not manufactured or calibrated with sufficient precision. If this is the case, you must level the tripod by holding the spirit level against the centre column instead of on the camera platform, and use the cross bubble rather than the one that runs the length of the level.

Choosing a lens for a panoramic series is not as simple as it might at first appear. Initially, you might think that a short focal length lens would be the best choice, since it takes in a wide angle of view and therefore reduces the number of exposures needed to make up the panoramic image. Unfortunately, this is not the case. A wide angle lens leads to

distortion where the pictures are joined. A standard lens or a short telephoto reduces the distortion to a minimum, but requires a larger number of exposures to be made.

If your subject has few straight lines in it, wide angle distortion might not matter, but generally there is something in the picture that draws attention to the join. For most purposes the practical minimum number of exposures for a 180° panorama is seven, each of which overlap at either side. By shooting pictures with more overlap than this, you increase your chances of finding a convenient line along which to cut and join two adjacent pictures. Some photographers leave so much overlap that a panorama could be made using just alternate frames from the sequence.

Arabic join-up *Imperfect matching of adjacent prints need not spoil a panorama. This example is made up of enprints, and the joins add rhythm to the picture, drawing attention to the moving figures*

Exposure and film

Once you have set up the camera and tripod, you have to make a decision about exposure. This is not entirely straightforward because it is likely that a meter reading which is appropriate when the camera is pointing in one direction will be inappropriate when it is turned through 90°, particularly if the sun appears in the scene. The solution to this problem is to select the area of the picture which is of principal interest, and to measure the exposure for this part of the scene. If possible, you should use a hand-held meter to take an incident light reading from the camera and under no circumstances should you allow the automatic system of your camera to set the shutter speed or aperture—this would lead to inconsistent exposure from frame to frame, and make printing more difficult. Setting one fixed value for exposure simplifies the printing stage.

The use of negative film also makes printing easier. Transparency film has less latitude to over- or underexposure, and this can lead to burnt-out highlights, or dark, empty shadows. Colour negative film also has the advantage that it can be processed by a standard printing service, to make a quick proof of the panorama.

If you are prepared to sacrifice the colour in the scene (or want to hand colour the picture) then you can use black and white film. Not only does this make the panorama much cheaper, but it eliminates colour matching, and therefore saves a lot of time in the darkroom.

When the time comes to actually make the exposures, work quickly, because the light can change surprisingly fast, particularly in the early morning and late afternoon. If there is a breeze, clouds can move quite quickly, and this can lead later on to some tricky cutting and matching if they travel too far across the frame between exposures.

The time between exposures is greatly increased if you try to bracket them in the normal way. Do this instead by making three consecutive 'sweeps' of the scene —first take a full panorama at the indicated exposure, then a complete one at one stop over, then a third at one stop under.

A motor drive or autowinder helps considerably in speeding up the process of shooting the panorama, and if you intend to produce many panoramic photographs, you may want to buy a panoramic tripod head—this has click stops at preset intervals so that you do not need to look through the viewfinder to line up the consecutive pictures.

Focusing the camera for a panorama is simple if the whole of your subject is a long way off. If there are no foreground features at all, focus on infinity. If there are some distant foreground objects, however, set the lens to its hyperfocal distance. Do this by moving the infinity symbol on the focusing scale until it is alongside the depth of field marking for the aperture in use. But if parts of the subject are ranged at different distances from the camera you should take extra pictures, with the lens set at a closer

focusing distance. For example, if a telephone box appears a few metres from the camera in one of the pictures, take an extra picture with the box in sharp focus, and then strip it separately into the final print.

Printing and joining

Printing and pasting together a panorama can be an expensive business, particularly if you are working in colour. For your first attempt, then, it is probably a good idea to use standard size prints. These are cheap, and for a trial run, they are ideal—they avoid the relatively tedious job of making eight or nine prints which may possibly prove unsuitable in the end. If your attempt at assembling this panorama is successful, you may then wish to make high quality prints yourself, or have the negatives hand-printed and colour matched by a professional laboratory.

If you are working in black and white and printing the pictures in your own darkroom, you should find it easy to match the density of adjacent prints, so

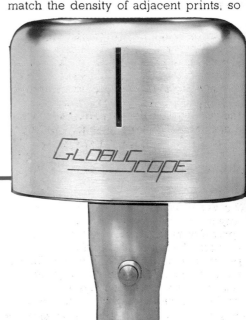

Panoramic cameras

Even in the early days of photography, panoramic cameras were popular, and there are still a number of them manufactured. Some, such as the Linhof Technorama, have a fixed ultra wide angle lens, and simply use a wider strip of film than usual to produce the panoramic image. Others, such as the Globuscope, form the wide picture by using a rotating camera body and a clockwork drive that moves the film across the focal plane in the course of the exposure. Finally, there is a third type of camera that has a pivoting lens. This moves rapidly through an arc when the shutter release is pressed, to take in a wide

angle of view. The Widelux camera is typical of this type.

All these three types of camera differ from each other, and from conventional cameras, mainly in the manner in which film is loaded. The Widelux, for example, has a curved film plane, and the Globuscope has a simple slit instead of a shutter. Both these two cameras use 35 mm film, whereas the Linhof Technorama takes four 180 × 60 mm photographs on each roll of 120 film.

In use, all three types have one thing in common—they must all be held perfectly level if distortion is to be avoided. This makes a tripod essential though any of the three can be hand-held if necessary. The Globuscope, however,

negative minimizes the effects of grain, which always shows up most prominently in areas of even tone.

Do not attempt any retouching on this first copy of the panorama, as the areas most in need of this are likely to be the joins, and the unevenness of the surface at these points makes the task almost impossible. Instead, make a copy print by photographing the first copy in good, even lighting and then retouch the copy print very carefully to disguise the joins in the panorama.

If you only want one copy of the panorama, this second generation image may be as far as you want to go, but if you aim to produce many identical prints of it, you will have to make a further copy negative by the same procedure. Since a certain amount of quality is lost each time an image is reproduced, you should use the largest size of film that you can at both copying stages—at least 120 roll film, and preferably 5 × 4 inch sheets.

Though this description will produce a conventional panorama, you can use it as a springboard for more imaginative projects. You might for example, choose to dispense with the tripod, for a free form panorama, or to point the camera steeply upwards so that the horizon curves round into a circle.

that there is not an abrupt change at the join. Try and print the images with slightly less contrast than usual, as the contrast inevitably rises when a copy negative is made, which is the next stage.

The procedure for cutting and joining the pictures is relatively straightforward. Since skies present special problems when it comes to matching together the individual pictures, you may choose to strip in a separate sky, rather than using the various portions of sky at the top of each picture. Some photographers make a point of photographing particularly attractive skies for this very reason—they accumulate a file of them for future use. If you have a medium format camera, use this for the purpose, because the sky negative needs a greater degree of enlargement than the negatives used for the piecemeal elements of the panorama. A larger format

Panoramic camera *The quick and easy way to take a panorama is to use a special camera. This one spins round when the button on the handle is pressed, and produces a long thin image on 35 mm film. Minimum coverage is 360°, and the camera will spin until the clockwork motor runs down*

spins through 360° in a little over a second, so that it photographs all its surroundings. This means that unless the photographer is to appear in the picture, he or she must hold the camera overhead, at arm's length.

In practical terms, a special camera is a much easier, quicker and more

efficient way of producing a panorama than the more pedestrian cut-and-paste approach. The major drawback is expense—the Linhof costs about four times as much as a professional quality 35 mm SLR. Consequently, many users, even professionals, prefer to hire such cameras rather than buy them.

Pictures in 3D

However clever the photographer is at exploiting perspective and the various visual clues to depth, there is no getting away from the fact that a photograph is two dimensional—or so it seems. But with two slightly different views of the same scene—a *stereo pair*—you can create a convincing illusion of depth using very simple techniques.

The camera sees the world from a single viewpoint, but our eyes form two separate images, each slightly different. These differences are 'decoded' by the brain, and interpreted as depth, so that we see the world in three dimensions. A stereo pair, by showing slightly different views, creates an illusion that is interpreted by the brain as depth. If we look at stereo pairs in such a way that each eye sees only one of the two, we can produce photographs which spring to life with remarkable realism.

The difference between the images that we see through each of our eyes is caused by their separation—usually about 65 mm. To reproduce these differences on film, we need to be able to take two pictures from viewpoints separated by a similar distance.

There are two major ways of achieving this separation. The simplest is to take two pictures in sequence, moving the camera between exposures. This method requires no special equipment, but is only suitable for static subjects. If the subject is moving, it is necessary to make the two exposures simultaneously. This can be done by using two linked cameras, a special camera with two lenses, or a conventional camera with a beam-splitter attachment.

Sequential exposures

The simplest way to take stereo pairs is to hand-hold the camera, and make a calculated guess about how far to move it between exposures. This is called *sequential* exposure.

Stand with your feet slightly apart, and take most of the weight of your body on one foot, before pressing the shutter for the first exposure. Then transfer your weight to the other foot, and make the second exposure. This should produce just sufficient stereo separation.

This may sound rather unreliable, but it is exactly the same technique as was used by the Apollo astronauts on the surface of the moon. Its lack of sophistication is more than compensated for by its convenience.

For good results using this and the more elaborate methods, certain precautions are essential. It is important that

the same part of the subject is centred in the viewfinder for both pictures, and that the camera is held at the same height and angle. Any distortion that is present is more obvious in stereo pictures than in conventional ones, and for this reason, it is better to use a standard, or slightly longer focal length lens to minimize distortion.

Use the smallest aperture that you can, because out of focus areas look very objectionable when viewed stereoscopically. Grain looks very odd as well, so use the finest grain film that is practical in the circumstances.

Avoid scenes with heavy shadow areas if possible, because the shadows may reduce the feeling of realism. High contrast pictures also look unnatural in stereo, but pictures which would normally be dismissed as lacking contrast often look perfectly normal when viewed as stereo pairs. Aim to produce as much detail as possible in all parts of the picture.

Concentrate the most interesting part of the subject in the foreground, but no closer than about one and a half metres to the camera. Subjects closer than this appear so widely separated in the final

Niagara. Ice Cave under the American Falls.

Stereo viewers *Essential for slides and a great help for prints, stereo viewers make it a great deal easier to combine the two stereo images*

pictures that the eyes cannot interpret them properly, while extremely distant subjects appear to have little depth.

Sequential stereo photography is made easier by using a tripod and some sort of slide mechanism, which then allows the camera to be moved the necessary distance without changing its alignment or direction. The focus slides which are designed for use with bellows are ideal, because they are usually have calibrations in millimetres marked on them and this helps to accurately set the stereo separation.

Simultaneous exposures

If you have two identical cameras, or can borrow a second camera that has the same focal length lens as your own, you can make both exposures at the same moment. This is very much easier if the two cameras are mounted on the same tripod, or on a bracket for hand-holding.

The bracket need not be particularly sophisticated, and could easily be put together from scraps of timber or metal. It should hold the cameras rigidly together, with the centres of the lenses about 65 mm apart. The shutter release can be linked by a bar so that both are pressed at once, or a double cable release can be used to coordinate the moment of exposure.

In the past, many specially designed stereo cameras have been available. They had linked lenses and shutters, and the apertures were specially calibrated to be perfectly matched. Only a few models are still manufactured, but secondhand stereo cameras can often be bought very cheaply.

A few camera manufacturers, notably Pentax, make a special accessory for

3D—the future

Stereo photography used to be more popular than it is today, but it seems likely that it will soon enjoy a resurgence of interest. Two recent developments may well revolutionize the field. The first is 'Holography', a sophisticated technology which produces remarkably lifelike images in 3D. Holograms need expensive equipment and enormous care in the making, but a good one is quite unlike any other kind of photograph.

To see the depth in a hologram, you need no special viewer, and the effect is rather similar to that of looking through a window at the original object. Unfortunately, however, there are a few limitations to the process: the plates that are used are very insensitive, and it is presently difficult to photograph moving objects directly. Holograms in true colour are not at present possible either, but both these obstacles may be removed by research. The full potential of holography is only just beginning to be exploited

The other development is likely to affect the amateur photographer more directly. It is a camera now manufactured by the Nimslo corporation, and it has four similar lenses mounted in a row on the front, and takes four images side by side on conventional 35 mm colour negative film. The camera is a non-reflex automatic model, and works well in conditions which also suit conventional point-and-shoot counterparts. Apart from the camera's unusual appearance, the main departure from conventional photography is in the printing of the pictures. After processing, the images from the four negatives are computer processed, and printed in narrow strips on a special paper. The surface of this is embossed with tiny lenticular prisms, which present each of the viewer's eyes with the appropriate image, thereby giving an illusion of three dimensions. No special viewer is needed to look at the pictures, and the only limitation is that the film must be processed by the camera's manufacturer.

3D souvenir *In Victorian times, stereo photography enjoyed a surge of popularity, and card mounted pairs like this often turn up in antique shops*

stereo photography. This is a beam splitter that is screwed to the front of the camera lens. It uses front-silvered mirrors and a prism to produce a stereo pair on a single frame of 35 mm film. Some of these attachments can also be used for viewing the image.

Viewing stereo pairs

Either negative or slide film can be used for taking stereo photographs, but unless you want to project the images, prints are probably more convenient to look at. For technical reasons, they should be no wider than about 65 mm, and should ideally be mounted side by side on card, so that the picture taken with the camera on the left is mounted on the left, and the right hand image on the right.

It is possible, with practice, to view stereo pairs directly. Place them on an evenly illuminated surface, and view them from about 30 cm away. Allow your eyes to relax so that instead of seeing two images, you see three. The central one of the three is in stereo. You may find that placing a piece of card between the two pictures helps you to fuse them into one.

Many people have difficulty in viewing prints this way and find it easier to print one of the images in reverse, then view the pair using a mirror. This simultaneously creates a barrier between the two pictures so that each eye sees only one of them, and brings the reversed print back to normal. The pictures accompanying this article have been reproduced for this method of viewing.

Many different designs of viewers used to be available at times when

Viewing stereo pictures

Viewing in stereo *To see depth in a stereo pair, each of our eyes must only see one of the two pictures. The left eye sees the image taken by the left hand lens, and vice versa*

Holmes viewer *The old-fashioned wooden viewers achieve 3D by using two lenses which bring the pictures into focus, and a panel which stops each eye from seeing the other picture*

Using a mirror *You can see depth in the pictures below without a viewer if you look at the left hand image of the pair through an ordinary mirror, put you need a little practice*

Stereo subjects *Even the most mundane scene can make quite an interesting picture in stereo. A static subject can be shot twice with the same camera, but moving ones need special apparatus*

stereo photography enjoyed greater popularity than it does today. A few of these are still produced, and others turn up on the secondhand market very frequently. Most of them use two magnifying lenses, and have some device to prevent the left eye from seeing the right hand image, and vice versa. Practically any sort of viewer makes it simple to form a stereo image from the two halves of the pair, and a few companies still make viewers, usually out of plastic.

Colour transparencies can be viewed in a similar way to prints, but the lighting requirements are different, and 35 mm transparencies generally need some enlargement. This makes a viewer essential. However, transparencies have the advantage that they can be projected so that a group of people can view them simultaneously.

This in itself presents problems, because each member of the audience must see the left hand image with their left eye, and the right hand image with their right eye. Many solutions to the problem have been tried in the past, but the only practical one is to use two projectors to superimpose the two images on a special metallic screen. The two lenses are then covered by pieces of polarizing material, with the planes of polarization at right angles to each other. Everyone in the room wears polarizing spectacles, with the planes of polarization matching those of the projection lenses. Thus each eye sees only the appropriate image.

Although this system is by far the

At the other end of the scale, if you have access to a telescope, you may be interested in taking stereo pictures of the moon. The movement of the earth provides the separation in this case, and exposures must be several hours apart.

Although this technique requires special equipment, many stereo techniques are very simple and encourage experiments. Indeed, the beauty of stereo photography is that it is so straightforward, and is a simple way of adding an extra dimension to your pictures. No special equipment is really necessary, and additional expense only adds polish and ease of viewing to your stereo photographs.

Beam splitter *For moving subjects, you must either use a special stereo camera, or one of these beam splitter accessories. They fit on to the front of a standard lens, and produce two vertical format pictures side by side on a conventional 35 mm frame. A matching viewer unites the images*

simplest, it has certain drawbacks. The polarizing filters cause a considerable light loss—about four stops—so the screen image is very dim. If the audience tilt their heads, the polaroid sheets cease be perfectly crossed, and each eye sees both images, causing eyestrain over long periods. For these reasons, stereo projection has never enjoyed great popularity, and the simple viewing of prints remains more practical.

Special techniques

When an object is very distant, each of our eyes receives an almost identical image, and we see very little depth in such a scene. Stereo photography offers the opportunity to enhance this feeling of depth, by increasing the distance between the points from which the two pictures of the stereo pair are taken. As a rough guide, the separation should be 1/50 of the distance to the closest object.

You could, for instance, photograph the view from the top of a high building. By taking two pictures from opposite corners on the same side of the building, you can make a stereo pair that shows each distant detail in dramatic relief. The impression produced on looking at the prints is similar to that of looking down on a model of the same scene.

Another application of this technique is stereo photography from the air. This is widely used for map making from special aircraft, but even a conventional passenger aircraft can be used to take oblique stereo photographs. The stereo separation is produced by the movement of the aircraft, but since this is so quick, a fast shutter speed has to be used, and the time that elapses between exposures must be very short. At average altitudes and speeds, no more than a second should elapse between exposures.

Pinhole pictures

Today many people think that you need a mass of technology in order to take good pictures. But in fact it is possible to take photographs using nothing more than a box with a tiny hole at one end and film at the other—a pinhole camera.

Indeed, pinhole cameras can be surprisingly versatile. You can use them to make a wide angle, long focus, zoom, multiple image, panoramic or even giant format pictures.

Pinholes produce soft, uniformly unsharp pictures with a quality all their own. Panoramic pinhole pictures are possible with a little DIY handicraft work, and you can even produce multi-image effects by piercing several closely spaced holes. 'Telephoto' pinholes are made simply by placing the hole a long way from the film. A zoom is created by fitting the pinhole to a bellows unit to vary the pinhole-to-film distance.

The camera body

Although the traditional pinhole camera is a simple home-made box, it is actually far easier to use an ordinary camera body for straightforward pinhole shots. Simply remove the lens and replace it with a home-made pinhole and expose in the normal way. This gives you a guaranteed light tight body and enables you to load the camera without retreating to the darkroom. A normal camera body is also far easier to work with.

The disadvantage of a camera body is that you cannot take ultrawide shots. The problem lies with the thickness of its body (about 40 mm). With the pinhole in position flat over the camera's lens throat, it will give an angle of view similar to that of a 40 mm lens. Only by placing the pinhole closer to the film can a really wide angle effect be produced. But unless your camera has a mirror lock you cannot do this.

A 35 mm rangefinder camera has a thinner body and no mirror. With its lens removed, a pinhole in a sunken mount can be pushed inside the throat to within a few millimetres of the shutter blinds, though if it is very close, the throat will restrict the field of view.

Both the SLR and the rangefinder bodies have built-in focal plane shutters. This makes exposing the film convenient and fully controllable. However, exposure times with pinholes are often very long—several seconds is common—so a shutter is far from essential. Other less sophisticated camera bodies without shutters can be used very successfully. Old, broken folding camera are par-

Daffodils *Pinhole optics, used here on 35 mm Agfachrome, have infinitely wide depth of field—or, alternatively, the definition is equally bad at all distances. The pinhole was 14 mm from the film for this shot*

ticularly good. With the lens, bellows and folding mechanism removed you are left with a very thin body and the freedom to place the pinhole as close to the film as you wish. But before starting such a drastic 'modification' make sure that the camera is expendable and that it takes a currently available film size. The 120 size offers the widest choice of emulsion types in roll film.

Other cameras worth considering for similar treatment include peel-apart Polaroid and 126 cartridge-load types. The 126 cartridge can even be used on its own providing a light-proof panel or box is fitted to the front.

All sorts of boxes and tins can be used to form the basic body. A round biscuit tin cut in half across the diameter makes an ideal basis for a panoramic camera. All you have to add is a front panel with a pinhole in the middle. For really huge pictures try a plastic dustbin!

Great precision is never required in any of these constructions—stiff card and hardboard are suitable materials. To make the camera lightproof, tape over all joints with at least two thicknesses of black insulating or carpet tape and paint all interior surfaces matt black. Cement a ¼ inch Whitworth nut to the base of your 'biscuit tin' camera, this allows you to fix the camera to a tripod.

Home-made cameras have to be loaded in a darkroom or changing bag. If you want the freedom to take several pictures on location, make sure that you have a changing bag large enough to accommodate the camera and two light-proof containers—one for exposed and one for unexposed materials.

Choosing the film

The best type of film to use for home-made pinhole cameras is sheet film, as this is easiest to handle. It is available in sizes from 5 × 4 inches (12.7 × 10.2 cm) to 40 × 30 inches (101.6 × 76.2 cm). Unfortunately, sheet film is very expensive. For panoramic pictures you can use roll film, detaching it from its paper backing, and taping the actual film in place around the curved inside of your camera. You can also use short lengths of 35 mm film.

For giant shots, you can use paper instead of film. Exposing on to black and white printing paper produces a negative image—this must be contact printed on to normal b & w print paper to give a positive print. Ordinary black and white printing paper can be used for the exposure, but it will distort some tonal values since it is only sensitive to ultraviolet and blue light. Panalure II RC paper is a panchromatic black and white paper designed for colour negatives and this gives better results, in particular recording red, green and orange colours at about their correct tonal values. The print may be made on conventional paper since the negative has the correct tones.

For giant colour pictures, try Cibachrome or Ektachrome R14 paper. These materials are balanced to give accurate colour in tungsten illumination, so if you use them in daylight you must fit an 85B filter. Other filters may be required to give completely accurate colour and you should experiment to achieve the right results. Both Cibachrome and Ektachrome papers give a direct positive image so no further print stage is needed. However, you must remember that an image formed in this way is laterally reversed—like looking into a mirror.

Exposure and filtration are best determined by a practical test. Take exposure meter readings at the same time and record all data. Once you have achieved a good result you can relate meter reading to actual exposure given for future reference. Printing paper should be processed promptly.

Making the pinhole

Once you have decided on the size of camera and the angle of view, you can set about making the actual pinhole.

For every pinhole-to-film distance (the equivalent of focal length in a lens) there is an optimum size for the hole. Make the pinhole larger than this size and the image becomes brighter, but less sharp. Make the hole smaller than the optimum and sharpness still deteriorates due to diffraction and the image gets darker. Details of the calculations involved and a list of optimum sizes is given in the 'Optimum pinhole size' box.

The hole should be perfectly circular and made in very thin material. The edges of the hole must be free from all fibres or fragments. Black card can be used, pierced with a hot needle to burn off any fine fibres at the edge of the hole. But metal foil is a better material to work with.

You need, in addition to the foil, scissors, centrepunch, a small hammer,

1 *A round biscuit tin can be turned into a good panoramic pinhole camera. Begin by cutting the tin in two using tinsnips, as shown here*

2 *The inside of the tin, including half the lid, should be painted matt black. This paint is sometimes called 'camera black' or blackboard paint*

3 *Make the front of the camera from stout black card. It can be stuck on using black carpet tape, which also forms the hinge for the lid*

4 *The pinhole must be made in a very thin material. Baking foil is often used, as it can be taped to the centre of the card camera front*

5 *In the dark, tape a sheet of photographic paper (emulsion outwards) to the curved inside of the camera. Tape the lid on securely*

6 *The shutter is simply a piece of black tape, stuck back to back at the centre to prevent it from damaging the pinhole. Use a secure base*

a whetstone, a fine needle, and a flat piece of wood or metal with a hole about 6 mm across in it.

Cut a piece of foil about 20 mm square. Place it over the hole in the wood and tap it gently with the centrepunch. Use only enough pressure to make a shallow dent in the middle. Gently rub the 'bump' side of the foil in the whetstone to reduce its thickness. Push the extreme point of the needle into the centre of the dented surface to make a minute hole. Turn the foil over and push the needle in from the other side, rotating it slowly. Keep the needle upright and use minimum pressure.

You now have to measure the diameter of the hole to establish the taking aperture. This is best done with the aid of an enlarger. Tape the foil to a slide mount and place it in the enlarger. Focus the image of the hole using the

Panoramic pinhole
This was taken using the camera shown under construction on the previous page. The material used was Ektachrome R14 reversal paper which required an 85B filter to balance it to daylight. A 15 second exposure was needed

maximum degree of enlargement possible. Check the shape of the hole and measure the diameter of its image. Remove the foil and replace it with a clear plastic rule, or piece of film marked with a centimetre scale. Using a second rule on the baseboard, measure the size of the projected scale—this gives you the degree of enlargement directly. Divide the diameter of the pinhole image by the degree of enlargement and you have the actual size of the pinhole.

Compare this figure with a scale for optimum pinhole sizes (see panel). Providing your pinhole is within 15 per cent of this figure, it is of the right diameter.

Having chosen a 'focal length', made a pinhole and measured its diameter,you can now work out its f-number. Simply divide pinhole-to-film distance by the diameter of the hole. For example, if your 'focal length' is 30 mm and the pinhole's diameter is 0.24 mm then the f-number is 30 divided by 0.24 which equals f/125.

Once you have made a satisfactory pinhole, glue or tape the foil in place. A sheet of stiff black card with a central hole makes an adequate panel. Cut to the appropriate size and shape, this can be fitted directly to the front of the camera body and lightproofed with

black tape. Paint the rear of the foil matt black, but take care not to fill part of the pinhole with paint.

Viewfinder

You do not need to focus a pinhole—every part of the subject is recorded equally unsharply. But although some of the pleasure of working with pinhole cameras comes from the unpredictability of the results, you may want some form of viewfinder to help compose the picture. With an SLR body used in bright daylight (with mirror down) it is just about possible to see an image on the screen. All other types of pinhole camera need an accessory finder.

An optical viewfinder like those sold for rangefinder cameras can be used. Even if it does not show the exact field of view it helps in aligning the camera with the centre of the subject area.

A more accurate viewfinder is easily made by constructing an open frame the same size as your film format. This frame is then viewed via a central 'peephole', positioned behind it at a distance equal to the pinhole-to-film 'focal length'.

To align the viewfinder on the camera body, shoot a test film with the camera firmly fixed in place. It is best to use black and white film because this can be processed straight away to allow an immediate check.

Sprocket shot
If you use 35 mm film the image will overlap the sprockets and edge markings. Rather than crop these out during printing, you can include the full area to produce an unusual and interesting image. This picture is of an interior and, without a pinhole camera, would have required a fisheye lens for the same coverage

Exposure techniques

If you are using a camera body, you can use the camera's shutter; if you are using a home-made camera, you can make the exposure simply by removing a cover from the pinhole and replacing it after the specified time—a lens cap makes an ideal 'shutter' cover.

When shooting on ordinary black and white film, exposure can be determined with a hand-held meter. However, it is quite possible that the scale on your meter does not include the effective aperture of the pinhole. To overcome this problem, you can use the following technique.

Take a meter reading in the normal way. Note the exposure time at f/16, then calculate the reduction in exposure time by counting how many stops smaller your pinhole is than f/16. The full sequence of f-numbers up to f/512 is: 16, 22, 32, 45, 64, 90, 128, 180, 256, 360.

If your pinhole has an aperture of f/128, for example, then the exposure time must be increased by a factor of six in comparison to the exposure time of f/16—f/128 is six stops smaller than f/16. Since each stop is a change in exposure of ×2, six stops is $2 \times 2 \times 2 \times 2 \times 2 \times 2$—that is, 64-times greater exposure.

So the exposure time at f/128 is 1/15 second × 64 — four seconds. Unfortunately, this exposure time may still not be correct. Most emulsions suffer from a loss of film speed at such long exposure times due to reciprocity law failure. So a further correction factor must be applied. This varies according to the length of exposure time and the characteristics of the film in use.

As a rough guide, for exposure times between one and ten seconds, apply the following factors—Ilford black and white × 2.5; Kodak black and white × 3.5; Kodak colour × 2.

With colour slide film you may also find there is an overall colour cast. Once a cast has been found, and clearly identified as being due to the long exposure, then it can be corrected in future photographs by filtration, though this requires even more exposure.

Slow tungsten balanced colour film is designed for long exposures and so hardly suffers from any loss of film speed at times of around ten seconds.

Optimum pinhole size

Optimum diameter for a pinhole depends on both the pinhole-to-film distance and the wavelength of light being used. Since photography is normally carried out in daylight, an average value is chosen.

Pinhole size is calculated as below:

$$D = 3.6 \times v \times W$$

Where: D = diameter of pinhole
v = pinhole-to-film distance
W = wavelength of light

The following table gives a list of likely pinhole-to-film distances (v), their optimum diameter (D) calculated from the formula, the f-number, N, of that combination and the factor by which an exposure time of f/16 must be multiplied.

v (mm)	D (mm)	N	Exposure factor
10	0.14	70	20
20	0.20	100	40
30	0.24	125	60
40	0.28	140	80
50	0.31	160	100
60	0.34	180	125
70	0.37	190	140
80	0.40	200	160
90	0.42	214	180
100	0.45	220	190
150	0.54	280	300
200	0.63	318	400
250	0.70	360	500
300	0.78	380	560
350	0.84	418	700
400	0.89	450	800

Remember, though, that shooting in daylight with a film such as Agfachrome 50L or Ektachrome 50 Professional, you need to use an 85B filter. The extra exposure needed can be taken into account by adjusting the film speed dial on the exposure meter by the appropriate filter factor.

You may be tempted to avoid the loss of effective film speed on long exposures by starting out with a high speed emulsion such as Kodacolor 400 or Tri-X. In bright daylight, even with an aperture as small as f/128, your exposure time could be as short as ¼ second. This is a useful approach to take, but only if your camera has a shutter.

If you are using an improvized body without a shutter then such short exposures are impossible to time accurately. Here you should use a slow or medium speed film, possibly in conjunction with a neutral density filter, to give an exposure of four seconds or more.

When using a camera without a shutter, fix any filter required in place before you load the camera. Once loaded the lens cap shutter cannot be raised without exposing the film. If you need to change filters this has to be done inside a changing bag or darkroom.

With an ultra-wide angle pinhole image, the centre is much brighter than the edges or corners. Fortunately the effect is rather attractive, creating a strong bright centre of interest, while the dark edges help to 'hold in' the composition.

However, if you want to minimize the effect, give extra exposure when using negative film by at least doubling the estimated time. At the printing stage you can even up the density difference between centre and edge by 'burning in' the middle. With slide film a compromise exposure has to be found. In this case it is best to expose for the bright parts to avoid washed out highlights. Cameras with curved backs, used for panoramic pictures, do not have this problem as the pinhole to film distance is constant across the film.

Taking into account all the various problems and effects possible with a pinhole image, negative film offers the best all round performance especially for colour photography. Exposure latitude is greater than with slide film, but the main advantage is that density and colour quality can be finely adjusted at the print stage.

Because it always requires a long exposure time the pinhole camera is best suited to fairly static subjects. Landscapes are the obvious choice, though in bright light you can easily shoot portraits providing the subject remains moderately still. The pinhole picture is never crisply sharp so any slight blurring is masked by the overall softness.

It is worth exploiting the long exposure to produce pictures which use blur and image movement creatively. To take a simple example, moving tree branches and rippling reflections on water will both record as indistinct images. With the right choice of subject both effects can lend an air of mystery or strangeness to an otherwise mundane scene. And with a pinhole camera, these effects are achieved simply and cheaply.

Multiple images
Effects that would normally require special filters are easy to produce with a pinhole camera. The picture above was taken in a single exposure using eight pinholes instead of just one. The separation of each image on the negative is the same as the separation between the pinholes.
Abbey ceiling
Almost any type of container can be used to make a pinhole camera. Distortions were created here by placing the pinhole in the curved surface of a cylinder

INDEX